WALK

HUMBLY

WITH

YOUR

GOD

SIMPLE STEPS TO A VIRTUOUS LIFE

Fr. Andrew Apostoli, C.F.R.

SERVANT
BOOKS

PUBLISHED BY ST. ANTHONY MESSENGER PRESS
CINCINNATI, OHIO

Cover design by Steve Eames
Cover photo by Andreas Vitting/istockphoto
Book design by Mark Sullivan

LIBRARY OF CONGRESS CATALOGING-IN-PUBLICATION DATA

Apostoli, Andrew.
  Walk humbly with your God : simple steps to a virtuous life / Andrew Apostoli.
    p. cm.
  ISBN 0-86716-759-9 (pbk. : alk. paper) 1. Christian life—Catholic authors. I. Title.

BX2350.3.A64 2006
248.4'82—dc22

                        2006012042

ISBN-13 978-0-86716-759-7
ISBN-10 0-86716-759-9
Copyright ©2006 Andrew Apostoli. All rights reserved.

Published by Servant Books, an imprint of
St. Anthony Messenger Press.
28 W. Liberty St.
Cincinnati, OH 45202
www.ServantBooks.org

Printed in the United States of America.

Printed on acid-free paper.

08 09 10 5 4 3

CONTENTS

+

JMJF

Some of the chapters of this book were written over a number of years for *Envoy* magazine. One such article was "The Lessons I Learned at Ground Zero." I wanted to use it as the introduction to this book because during the course of our lives all of us encounter significant challenges, a fact that the events of September 11, 2001, brought into sharp focus. To meet any challenge effectively, we need to be faithful to prayer, practice the virtues and develop our understanding of how suffering is a sharing in the cross of Christ. Whether our challenges are big or small, living a faithful Christian life will enable us to persevere and win the crown of eternal life with Christ.

ACKNOWLEDGMENTS

A s a writer, I have felt a strong desire to share from my own study, reflection and experiences whatever might help my brothers and sisters in Christ along their spiritual journey through life. Many people contributed their advice and expertise, though, to help this book become a reality. I would like to gratefully acknowledge them.

First, I wish to thank Patrick Madrid for permission to use articles I wrote on prayer and charity for *Envoy* magazine. Next, I would like to thank Lou Cortese and St. Joseph Radio for permission to transcribe a series of tapes from a retreat I gave at Sacred Heart Retreat House in Alhambra, California, on the meaning of suffering in the Christian life.

I am also grateful to Elaine Curzio and Maryann Anderson for transcribing the taped talks. Finally, I would like to thank Cindy Cavnar and the editors at Servant Books for their work to bring this book to print.

The title of this book comes from the words of the prophet Micah. They have long had a special appeal to me: "You have been told, O man, what is good, / and what the LORD requires of you: / Only to do the right and to love goodness, / and to walk humbly with your God" (Micah 6:8, NAB). May all the love and care that so many have poured into the preparation of this book enable all of us to walk humbly with our God!

FATHER ANDREW APOSTOLI, C.F.R.

• The Lessons I Learned at Ground Zero •

September 11, 2001, has profoundly affected all of us, not only in the United States of America but throughout the world. It is a date never to be forgotten. The events of that day were truly catastrophic, involving as they did the mass murder of innocent people, the indescribable sorrow of those who so suddenly lost loved ones and the destruction of institutions of great symbolic importance to the American people. We must then add to all these events a resultant fear of terrorism that has gripped America. As a nation we were almost oblivious to such fear, but now we find it threatening the very foundation of our American way of life, namely, our sense of freedom and security.

Such events, however, make us face even deeper issues. They thrust us instinctively into the sphere of faith and make us ask once more those fundamental questions: Where does such evil come from? Why does God permit it? Can any good come out of an evil like this? Can we prevent it, and if so, how? These and many more questions flood our minds and hearts at this time.

On Friday, October 5, the effects of September 11 on the World Trade Center became very real for me as I found myself at Ground Zero. Many of my confreres in the Franciscan Friars of the Renewal had been able to get down close to that area soon after the tragedy. They were able to offer some material help to needy people, but mostly they offered spiritual assistance to the many volunteers searching for victims and removing the debris. They offered the consolation of their prayers and comforting words to those who were either still searching for the whereabouts of missing loved ones or to those who had received word that their loved ones had indeed died in the tragedy.

Our Franciscan Sisters of the Renewal were also close to the devastated area. They told of visiting hospitals to console the injured and to pray with distraught family members. They passed out rosaries, holy cards and medals. Everyone took something, no matter what his or her religious beliefs, if any. People were desperately reaching out to find something that could give consolation in their suffering, hope in their despair and faith in their darkness! When every rosary, holy card and medal was gone, the Sisters never stopped giving their prayers.

My opportunity to minister at Ground Zero came when the Archdiocese of New York, in conjunction with other surrounding dioceses, put out an appeal for priests to minister at the morgue that was set up at Ground Zero.

Two priests were assigned to this ministry twenty-four hours a day for as long as they were needed. When I volunteered, I was assigned to an eight-hour shift beginning at 6:00 AM on October 5. The priest assigned with me had once been a student of mine at St. Joseph's Seminary in the Dunwoodie section of Yonkers, New York.

Before we could go down to the disaster site, we had to report to a fire department command post for a briefing. We were told by volunteer firefighters (who had come from out-of-state to help out during the disaster) that the site was actually far worse than could be seen through the media. We were told that we were to offer prayers over the remains of victims who had been recovered from the rubble, and then to offer prayers for the volunteers who brought in the recovered bodies.

What they next told us made a deep impression on me. The firefighters and the police follow a certain code: "You go in together, you come out together!" They said that if a body of a firefighter or a police officer was recovered, there would be a special ritual. The rescue workers would stop working in that area. One of the priests would be called to the disaster site to bless the body where it was recovered and to bless the spot as well. Then the body would be transported to the morgue with an honor guard of fellow firefighters or police officers.

Around eight o'clock during our tour of duty at the morgue, the body of one of the firefighters was found. The other priest was called to the site, where he offered prayers for the deceased firefighter and blessed the spot where he had fallen in service. I was at the morgue when his body was brought in with an honor guard of comrades. The firefighter's body was transported on a small utility vehicle. It had been placed on a bier and draped with an American flag. The honor guard consisted of six firefighters, three on each side of the body.

I do not think I will ever forget the impression this little cortege made on me as I watched it coming slowly up the road from the disaster site to the morgue. The little vehicle had its lights on, moving through a hazy cloud of smoke coming from the constantly burning fires at the wreckage site. The men who formed the honor guard, now involved in the clean up operation, were covered head to foot with dirt and grime. Despite their appearance, the looks on their faces reflected a combination of sorrow at carrying out one of their own, and a deep sense of respect and admiration for one of their fallen heroic comrades. The words of Jesus came instinctively to mind: "Greater love has no man than this, that a man lay down his life for his friends" (John 15:13).

Throughout the remainder of my time at Ground Zero, I met many wonderful and generous volunteers who had come from far and near to offer their time, talent and supplies for whatever was needed. There was an outpouring of generous love and concern by so many in the face of this enormous tragedy. There were many opportunities to speak with various firefighters, police officers and rescue workers, and the overwhelming majority were quite open to the message of faith and trust in God. One man told me how much his Catholic faith meant to him in the face of such suffering. The crisis had brought people together and had also brought about a blessed moment for the new evangelization.

There is one final experience I would like to share. A Salvation Army truck had been set up to provide coffee, cake, water, soda and many other snacks for all those involved in the recovery operation. I was having a cup of coffee there when I met a woman wearing a jacket with the initials EMT (Emergency Medical Technician) clearly on the back. We began to talk about the big steel cross that had been set up near the entranceway to the heart of Ground Zero. I had seen a picture of it in an article in one of the New York City newspapers.

Some of the firefighters, when entering what remained of a smaller building that had burned and collapsed, had seen this huge steel formation of a cross perfectly intact. As we were talking about the cross, she told me that the firefighters who discovered the cross were telling everyone at the site to go see it. Many did but she was afraid to go the first day. Finally, she got up the courage to go and see the cross. This is basically how she described her experience: "I went into the building. There was the large cross. But behind it were three smaller crosses. The light of the sun was just beginning to break into the building, coming in right behind the crosses!" Then she said to me, "I hate to tell you this, but it all looked so beautiful!" I responded to her, "It is the presence of the cross that gives all this any meaning."

Later, some steelworkers removed the cross and transferred it to a place of prominence. Every person walking in and out, every truck moving in and out, passed the cross.

When we go through a tragedy like September 11, we sincerely ask: "Can any good ever come from this evil?" I believe we have to trust that God would not permit an evil to happen except to draw a greater good from it. Obviously, the original sin of our first parents was the greatest tragedy the human race ever experienced. Yet Saint Augustine called it a "happy fault" because it merited for us so great a Savior! I experienced some of that greater good in the generosity and courage of the firefighters and police officers who gave their lives in what can only be called a heroic manner. I saw it further in the generous sharing of countless volunteers. It was present in the prayers and trust of those who were hurting and of those who were ministering to them. Ultimately, it was seen in the cross at Ground Zero that proclaimed not death but the hope and the victory of eternal life in Jesus Christ!

PART ONE

• PRAYER AND THE LIFE OF VIRTUE •

• P R A Y   A L W A Y S .   J E S U S   D I D !   •

Anyone intent on living as a sincere and dedicated Christian must take prayer seriously. All the saints had a great conviction about the importance of prayer. A man who is very devoted to Saint Padre Pio and knew him personally told me how important prayer was to this great saint. Shortly before his death, Padre Pio's superior asked him what he would like to have written on his tombstone. The Padre answered, "Write: 'Here lies a friar who prayed!'" And pray he did, especially the rosary, from morning until night. It is no wonder he was able to touch so many souls and lead them closer to Jesus and Our Lady.

Lack of prayer, on the other hand, will inevitably bring disastrous consequences for anyone claiming to be a follower of Christ. Without it, the Christian experience will often become shallow and meaningless. Why? Because if someone does not know Jesus Christ personally—a relationship that develops through prayer—then the Mass and all the sacraments will simply deteriorate into empty rituals.

This is why so many young people are turned off by the Mass and fail to appreciate its infinite value. Anyone who works with teenagers has heard the complaint: "I'm not going to Mass. It's boring! I don't get anything out of it!" Many of these young people end up leaving the Catholic Church. Some leave for good while others return only after they find Jesus personally in their lives—often through Scripture reading and prayer—and then realize it is the same Jesus who is present in the Mass. As Archbishop Fulton J. Sheen used to say, many people don't get anything out of Mass because they don't put anything into it. This includes prayer.

Christians who don't pray will tend to have their faith experience become nothing more than a search for pious feelings. We don't want to be Christians who merely feel good; that would be equivalent to a kind of spiritual gluttony. Nor do we want to be Christians who simply look devout; that would amount to nothing more than spiritual hypocrisy. Without prayer, and a steady dose of it, we won't strive to root out our sins and sinful attachments, nor will we expend any worthwhile efforts to practice the daily virtues, such as patience, trust, kindness, purity and obedience.

The only legitimate conclusion we can arrive at is that not only must we pray regularly but also, in the words of the Gospel, we must "pray always" (Luke 18:1, NRSV). If we need convincing, we have only to look at the example of Our Lord Himself who prayed—and He prayed always. We see this most clearly in the Gospel of Luke because prayer is one of his favorite themes. For example, Saint Luke gives us Our Lady's beautiful canticle of praise and thanksgiving, the Magnificat (see Luke 1:46–55). In the infancy narratives, he shows us great lives of prayer as reflected in Zechariah and Elizabeth, the parents of Saint John the Baptist; Simeon, whose life was open to the guidance of the Holy Spirit; and Anna, the prophetess who spent her days fasting and praying in the temple (Luke 1, 2).

But most of all, Saint Luke frequently stresses the fact that *Jesus* prayed. He prayed at significant moments in His life, such as His baptism: "Jesus also had been baptized and was praying" (Luke 3:21); and His transfiguration: "He took with him Peter and John and James, and went up on the mountain to pray. And as he was praying, the appearance of his countenance was altered" (Luke 9:28–29).

He spent long periods of time in prayer or went to solitary places to pray. Before Jesus chose the apostles, "he went out into the hills to pray; and all night he continued in prayer to God. And when it was day, he called his disciples, and chose from them twelve, whom he named apostles" (Luke 6:12–13). Jesus loved solitude: "He would withdraw to deserted places and pray" (Luke 5:16, NRSV); "Jesus was praying alone, with only the disciples near him" (Luke 9:18, NRSV).

He had a powerful influence on others not only in terms of his healing or his preaching, but also by his striking example and teaching on how to pray: "He was praying in a certain place, and when he ceased, one of his disciples said to him, 'Lord, teach us to pray, as John taught his disciples.' And he said to them, 'When you pray, say: Father, hallowed be thy name'" (Luke 11:1-2).

Jesus also prayed in moments of great intensity, such as His agony in the garden:

> He came out and went, as was his custom, to the Mount of Olives; and the disciples followed him. When he reached the place, he said to them, "Pray that you may not come into the time of trial." Then he withdrew from them about a stone's throw, knelt down, and prayed, "Father, if you are willing, remove this cup from me; yet, not my will but yours be done." Then an angel from heaven appeared to him and gave him strength. In his anguish he prayed more earnestly, and his sweat became like great drops of blood falling down on the ground. When he got up from prayer, he came to the disciples and found them sleeping because of grief, and he said to them, "Why are you sleeping? Get up and pray that you may not come into the time of trial." (Luke 22:39–46, NRSV)

What Did Jesus Pray for?

Jesus' prayers had many purposes or themes, such as:

- praise and joy: "At that same hour Jesus rejoiced in the Holy Spirit and said, 'I thank you, Father, Lord of heaven and earth, because you have hidden these things from the wise and the intelligent and have revealed them to infants'"(Luke 10:21, NRSV);

- intercession: "Simon, Simon, behold, Satan demanded to have you, that he might sift you like wheat, but I have prayed for you that your faith may not fail; and when you have turned again, strengthen your brethren" (Luke 22:31–32);
- forgiveness for his persecutors: "And Jesus said, 'Father, forgive them; for they know not what they do'" (Luke 23:34);
- anguish and sorrow: "My God, my God, why have you forsaken me?" (Matthew 27:46, NRSV).
- entrustment of Himself to His Father: "The curtain of the temple was torn in two. Then Jesus, crying with a loud voice, said, 'Father, into thy hands I commit my spirit!' And having said this he breathed his last" (Luke 23:45–46).

Much more could be said about the important place prayer had in the life of Jesus as demonstrated in the Gospel of Luke and in the other Gospels as well. Do yourself a favor and read through those passages, letting the Lord's own example convict you of the necessity to pray always. He did!

Devotion to the Holy Eucharist is at the very heart of Catholic life. In his first message to the Church after his election, Pope Benedict XVI said that the Eucharist is "the heart of Christian life and the source of the Church's evangelizing mission."[1] As we know, Pope John Paul II also frequently emphasized the Church's Eucharist-centered spirituality. In fact, he died during the Year of the Eucharist, a time he had set aside for the Church to focus its attention on this sacrament, the center of our faith.

Every Catholic needs the vitality, wisdom and strength that come forth from Jesus in the Holy Eucharist. Whether encountering the Lord for the first time in conversion, returning to the Lord after leaving the faith or encountering him daily in faithful, ongoing conversion, every true Catholic will end up at the tabernacle.

Encountering the Living Christ

What does it mean to encounter the living Christ? Let's take a look at the experience of the apostle Andrew when he first meets Jesus. Andrew and another unnamed disciple—traditionally, the apostle John—are disciples of John the Baptist. When the Baptist announces Jesus as the Lamb of God, they leave John and begin to follow Jesus. Our Lord, seeing them following Him, turns and asks, "What do you seek?" "Where are you staying?" they respond. "Come and see," Jesus answered. So they went to see where He was staying and remained with Him that day. I like to think of this as the first holy hour "plus"!

What follows? "He [Andrew] first found his brother Simon, and said to him, 'We have found the Messiah.'... He brought him to Jesus" (see John 1:35–42). Andrew would not have known who Jesus was unless the Baptist had first pointed Him out and Andrew himself had *spent time in a personal encounter with Jesus.* Nor would he have known where to bring his brother, Simon, unless he knew from *personal experience* where Jesus could be found. Once they encountered the Lord, Jesus took over their formation in discipleship. Our own living encounter with Jesus, especially in a eucharistic holy hour, will have similar effects for us.

A eucharistic holy hour is exactly as its name implies: an hour spent in prayer before Jesus in the tabernacle. Archbishop Fulton J. Sheen was one of the twentieth century's greatest apologists and evangelists, as well as the National Director of the Society for the Propagation of the Faith for sixteen years. He was so convinced of the importance of the eucharistic holy hour for his life and ministry that he made a holy hour daily for over fifty years, despite a demanding schedule and worldwide travel. He called it, fittingly, the "hour of power."

A former secretary of the archbishop's told me that he always made his holy hour after breakfast. (Archbishop Sheen once said that people should never try to make a holy hour before they've had their first cup of coffee!) He then spent additional time near the chapel writing, drawing his inspiration from our Lord in the Eucharist. When people congratulated him for his fine speaking and writing, telling him that he was very talented, he always answered that he had no such talent. He said that the power of his words, written and spoken, came from Jesus in the Blessed Sacrament.

The Hour of Power in a Broken World

Pope Benedict XVI, you will recall, stated that the Eucharist is "the source of the Church's evangelizing mission." Since that is the case, what will the hour of power do for us as we try to bring the Good News to those around us?

Time spent before the Eucharist deepens our personal encounter with Christ Himself. He becomes more real to us and our faith increases. This is important in evangelization because faith has two critical elements, belief and trust. As belief, faith is "the conviction of things not seen" (Hebrews 11:1). We do not see Christ in the Holy Eucharist with the eyes of our body, but with the eyes of faith we know and believe He is really present, body, blood, soul and divinity. To paraphrase Saint Thomas Aquinas's beautiful hymn, "Tantum Ergo": Faith will tell us Christ is present when our human senses fail.

Regarding trust, faith is "the assurance of things hoped for" (Hebrews 11:1). Once our faith moves us to believe in Jesus' real presence in the Blessed Sacrament, we also experience a growing desire for others to love him, even the whole world. Like Saint Andrew, after our personal stay with Jesus, we will lose no time going out and working to bring family, friends, strangers, and yes, even enemies of the Church, to Jesus.

None of us can introduce someone to a person we don't know or can't find. If we are rooted in eucharistic devotion, we know who Jesus is and where we can always find Him. As someone once put it, the measure of our holiness and effectiveness with others is the degree to which God becomes real in our lives. Where can Jesus become more real for us than in the Blessed Sacrament?

Going Forth

When we are before our eucharistic Lord, we should ask that He anoint our words, written and spoken, so that they convey the convincing power of the Spirit and not simply the wisdom of men (see 1 Corinthians 2:4–5). Furthermore, we must plead with Jesus so that those we evangelize are disposed to receive Him, His message and His Church.

Jesus' parable of the sower (Matthew 13:1–9, 18–23)

compares the human heart to soil that receives the planter's seed. Some of the seed falls on the path and the birds eat it; some falls on rocky ground and springs up quickly but just as quickly dies for lack of roots; some falls among thorns and is choked off; some falls on good soil. Using this parable as a guide, we should ask Jesus to open the hearts of those who are closed or resistant because they lack understanding (the "path" souls), to strengthen the hearts of those who are weak and inconsistent (the "rocky" souls), and to set free those held back by sinful attachments and addictions (the "thorn" souls). The seed has potential for a tremendous yield—as much as a hundredfold—but the soil where it lands makes all the difference.

Archbishop Sheen used to say that the hour of power drives from our hearts any spiritual mediocrity, laziness, indifference and fear. The fire of love in the eucharistic heart of Jesus will set our own hearts on fire with ardent love for Him. Then we will go with courage and conviction to bring the whole world to Jesus. Then will Jesus' desire come closer to fulfillment: "I came to cast fire upon the earth; and would that it were already kindled!" (Luke 12:49).

Jesus told Saint Faustina that there are two thrones of His mercy in the world: the tabernacle and the confessional. Jesus in the Eucharist sustains us in our daily lives and also sustains our work of evangelization by equipping us with the power of the Holy Spirit. Just as a power tool disconnected from its power source won't work, so the Catholic disconnected from the eucharistic Lord becomes ineffective. Countless demands and activities of all sorts sweep us along so that we easily become disconnected from the Lord. He will daily recharge the batteries of our life and ministry during the hour of power. As we pray before the tabernacle and maintain our living relationship with Jesus, we will find ourselves abundantly blessed and better able to communicate God's mercy to a broken world.

•   LORD, TEACH US HOW TO PRAY   •

Prayer is one of the most important things we can do because when we pray, we speak with God. Saint Augustine stressed the importance of this ongoing conversation when he pointed out that if we pray well, we will live well; if we live well, we will die well; and if we die well, all will be well. It's very important, then, to know how to pray well!

Just as our natural life on earth develops through different stages of growth such as childhood, adolescence and adulthood, so our spiritual life develops. This is evident as we pass through different stages of prayer. For example, in her spiritual masterpiece, *The Interior Castle*, Saint Teresa of Avila traced the soul's growth in holiness through seven "mansions" or dwelling places, each characterized by one or more forms of prayer.

Formal Prayer

While there are many stages of prayer, let's look at the one with which most of us are familiar: formal prayer, the prayer of beginners in the spiritual life. Beginners include young children who need to be taught their prayers along with everything else to equip them for life; recent con-verts, especially those with little or no religious back-ground; and certain simple people who lack the training or encouragement to advance on their spiritual journey. All these people are novices at prayer. Inexperienced in talking with God, at least in any depth, they often feel awkward when they try to do so. They need help regarding how and what to say when they speak to God in prayer. This is the purpose of formal prayer!

Scripture gives us an example of how to proceed when it presents the incident in which the disciples asked Jesus to teach them how to pray (Luke 11:1–4). He taught them a simple formal prayer—the most perfect of all prayers—the Our Father. Notice that He didn't teach them a tech-nique involving a certain posture or rhythm of breathing or a systematic method of meditation. Like most begin-ners, they were not ready for anything like that. They needed a no-frills approach, and that's exactly what the Lord gave them.

Formal prayer, as the word implies, involves a pre-set wording or formula that expresses what we want to say. Usually they are the words of someone else whom we feel was close to God and knew how to express thoughts that we feel unable to express ourselves. Often these prayers have a depth or beauty or inspirational quality that pulls us in and helps us draw near to God.

The Our Father, Hail Mary and Glory Be to the Father

are the most prominent of formal prayers. We use these constantly because they remind us of some of the most basic revealed truths. Other formal prayers include the Acts of Faith, Hope, Love and Contrition, the Morning Offering and grace before and after meals.

Many of our personally favorite prayers are formal prayers. The Peace Prayer of Saint Francis—"Lord, make me an instrument of your peace; where there is hatred, let me sow love…"—is a wonderful formal prayer that also motivates us to do good to others. The Memorare, the beautiful prayer to Our Lady, is a favorite formal prayer for many people. When you pray its inspiring introduction—"Remember, O most gracious Virgin Mary, that never was it known that anyone who fled to your protection, implored your help or sought your intercession, was left unaided…"—you know it's not possible for Our Lady to turn a deaf ear to your need. Many times in my own life, this prayer has inspired me to have great confidence. Although others wrote these prayers, in praying them we make them our own.

Lifting Our Minds and Hearts to God
How do formal prayers help us to pray? Saint John Damascene defined prayer as the lifting of the mind and heart to God. Formal prayers allow us to focus our minds on the meaning or content of the words, absorbing this meaning and making it our own. Simultaneously, the words stir up in our hearts feelings such as praise, hope,

love, courage and trust. As our minds grasp the words and our hearts are moved, both mind and heart are formed in sublime attitudes and sentiments. Ultimately, we grow in familiarity with God so that someday we will enjoy a confidence and ease in speaking to Him spontaneously.

This lifting of our minds and hearts to God is no doubt the great blessing of formal prayer. Ironically, it is also its greatest challenge. Most people praying formal prayers find themselves easily distracted. You're reciting the words of a formal prayer, for example, and trying to focus your mind and heart on their meaning. All of a sudden, your mind is thinking of a movie or baseball game you saw on television yesterday, or something you were supposed to do before you went to work or school but haven't done yet. Fears, anxieties or even joyful expectations flood your mind, taking the focus away from God. At the same time, they overwhelm those prayerful sentiments in the heart until you feel that you're totally empty of any sense of love, praise or trust.

When this happens, many people are tempted to give up praying. Don't do that! It would be a big mistake, and really, the situation is not as bad as it seems. If you find yourself in this position, remember a few pointers. First, distractions are natural. They come on their own. I have heard that the human mind cannot concentrate on something for more than twenty-five seconds without distraction! So expect distractions since they come from our human limitations and weakness.

Second, it is only when we willfully allow distractions into our minds that our prayer connection with God is actually broken. Involuntary distractions, those that come even though we do not want them, don't offend God. In a way, the heart's desire to love God continues even when the mind is elsewhere.

Third, when distractions do come, gently try to bring your mind and heart back into clear focus on God. Gently concentrate on the meaning of the words of your prayer and offer the sentiments of your heart to Him again. Try not to get frustrated or disturbed, for these will create even more distractions.

Fourth, if you are praying privately and the distractions are overwhelming, stop your prayers for a while and come back to them at another time when you are more settled. If you are praying with a group, just continue praying, and trust that your heavenly Father who sees in secret knows your trial and will reward your efforts.

A Rich Heritage

We will never outgrow our need for formal prayer. The liturgy, for instance, consists mainly of formal prayer. The sacraments, the rosary and such devotions as Saint Faustina's chaplet of Divine Mercy all utilize prayer formulas. The Liturgy of the Hours, also called the Divine Office, consists primarily of praying the 150 psalms of the Old Testament. God inspired the psalms as formal prayers that would provide a way for us to speak to Him confidently. The psalms, interestingly enough, do seem to cover every kind of life situation or human emotion we might encounter and want to talk to God about in prayer.

Formal prayer is sometimes known as vocal prayer because it is often prayed aloud; Eastern Christians refer to it as "the prayer of the lips." Some people use vocal prayer almost exclusively when they pray privately, feeling no need or desire to practice mental prayer. Saint Anthony Mary Claret said that vocal prayer suited him better than mental prayer because when he prayed prayers such as the Our Father and Hail Mary he sensed God's unfathomable mercy and goodness. He noted that God gave him many graces during mental prayer but it was during vocal prayer that he had a deeper awareness of God.

Saint Teresa of Avila says that some people have even reached the heights of perfection primarily using formal prayer. God gives His gifts as He chooses. But whoever uses formal prayer effectively has already taken the first step into a deeper relationship with the Lord.

• MENTAL PRAYER: AN IMPORTANT HELP
TO GROWTH IN HOLINESS •

If our spiritual life is going to develop properly, we must learn how to meditate, to practice mental prayer. What does this mean? When I entered the seminary, I discovered there were designated periods of mental prayer or meditation in the daily schedule. At first it sounded somewhat mystifying. "What is mental prayer? How do I meditate?" I wondered.

I was used to saying formal prayers, such as morning and night prayers, and some devotional prayers in a prayer booklet. But somehow the idea of mental prayer seemed complicated. I heard talk of different methods and steps in the meditation process. Every day in the chapel the community heard a reflection from a meditation book, and even this had many meditation points to consider. I felt a bit apprehensive!

After going to a few meditation periods, however, I realized that mental prayer came quite naturally. There was nothing to be afraid of. I began simply by thinking about Jesus in the Gospels, about His words and actions, or about some important part of my Catholic faith, like the Mass or God's mercy. Then I found myself wanting to talk to the Lord about my reflections. I came to realize that my thinking or reflecting (that's the actual meditation) was leading me to new insights about Jesus and the truths of the faith. These insights, in turn, were stirring up various feelings within me that are referred to as sentiments or affections. The more I meditated and came to new insights, the more I spoke with the Lord in my own words. It was like having a loving conversation heart-to-heart, mine with His.

In fact, I came to realize that I had actually been meditating for a long time—whenever I prayed the rosary, for example. When we recite any of the twenty decades of the rosary, we meditate on either the joyful, luminous, sorrowful or glorious mysteries that commemorate the significant events in the lives of Jesus and Mary. By constantly thinking about—meditating on—these mysteries when I prayed the rosary, they became more meaningful for me and I came to know more of Jesus' and Mary's love for me.

A similar thing happened when I made the Stations of the Cross. Meditating on fourteen scenes from the passion and death of our Lord, I experienced sentiments or affections of deeper gratitude to Jesus for all He suffered for me. I felt deeper sorrow for my sins, too, since they caused Jesus to suffer so much. This in turn moved me to be more resolved, with the help of His grace, not to commit these sins again in the future. Judging from my own experience, I would say that many Catholics first learn to meditate simply by reciting the rosary or making the stations.

Here are a few suggestions that might help as you move into mental prayer or meditation.

Mental prayer, also called the prayer of the mind, usually develops naturally from formal prayer or the prayer of the lips, as my own experience demonstrates. A comparison between these two types of prayer can be useful. As we know, Saint John Damascene defined prayer as the raising of the mind and the heart to God. In formal prayer, when we focus on the words of the prayer with our minds, the heart is then moved to love God with the sentiments contained in those words. If we recite an Act of Faith, for example, the words would logically stir up sentiments of faith, moving us to think: "God, you are all-knowing and you reveal to us what we need to know and do to get to heaven. I believe in all that you have revealed to us! Please grant me a strong faith so that I will always believe what you teach us through your Church!"

In mental prayer, however, the focus is not simply restricted by the words of a prayer formula. Rather, the focus is usually on a story, such as an event in the life of Jesus, or a teaching He gave, such as a parable, or something from the life of a saint or from reading a spiritual book. The mind is not limited to the words but moves through various details of the story or ideas contained in the teaching. By reflecting on these details, the mind can produce a far wider range of insights that stir more sentiments in the heart. The mind is freer to roam through this spiritual food for thought. The working of formal prayer and mental prayer is like the difference between reciting a poem where one is restricted to the words, and telling a story where the individual can elaborate in his or her own words.

Mental prayer has other benefits, including promoting a greater understanding of the teachings of our Catholic faith. Meditating leads us deeper into these realities and we discover insights that were not obvious at first sight. Saint John of the Cross describes this process as similar to mining for precious metals, like gold. If there's "gold in them there hills," then the more you mine, the more you'll find. The treasures of Scripture and other truths of our faith are not always obvious on the surface but they are limitless for those who dig for them.

Another benefit, as we have seen, is that our reflections stir up the vital sentiments of the heart so needed for loving and serving the Lord faithfully. These sentiments are really the most important fruit of mental prayer. They lead us to talk to God; without them we would end up in a purely intellectual exercise. Prayer requires this sort of conversation, and the sentiments are necessary to it. In this regard, we should mention that beginners practicing mental prayer do much more reasoning or reflecting in the mind than speaking from the heart. As time goes on, however, less reflection will be needed to procure more affection.

This is similar to the growth of a human friendship. When friends first meet, they ask a lot of questions and share many facts about themselves to get to know each other better. After the friendship has grown, however, there are fewer questions but a deeper knowledge and more intense mutual love. In fact, when the reasoning in prayer becomes significantly less and the sentiments in the heart begin to predominate, it is usually a sign one has come to the third stage of prayer, affective prayer or the prayer of the heart.

Finally, mental prayer helps us form the resolutions we need to grow in the love of God and neighbor through a conscious and consistent practice of Christian virtues. Our reflections, under the light of the Holy Spirit and with the assistance of His grace, give us insights on how to apply the values of the gospel, Church teachings and the wisdom of the saints to our own daily lives. Mental prayer is a must for growth in Christian holiness.

• DO YOU TALK TO GOD IN YOUR OWN WORDS? •

I once asked two women on different retreats, "Do you pray?" The first woman answered, "No, I talk to God in my own words." The second said, "Yes, I talk to God all day long." The understanding of prayer was different, but they were probably close to the same point on their spiritual journeys.

The first woman, in answering "No" to the question, "Do you pray?" apparently was limiting her idea of prayer to the use of a set formula of words that help us to talk to God. But her statement, "I talk to God in my own words," showed that she actually enjoyed a somewhat close, personal relationship with Him. She didn't recognize this informal, free, familiar conversing with God as genuine prayer, but it certainly was.

The second woman simply stated that she also had a close, personal prayer relationship with God: "I talk to God all day long." Unlike the first woman, though, she was aware of it as true prayer. She was comfortable speaking heart-to-heart with the Lord, sharing her thoughts and experiences with Him. This would indicate she had already achieved a certain degree of spiritual intimacy with God in daily loving dialogue.

Both women were experiencing the kind of prayer we call affective prayer or, as Eastern Christians say, the prayer of the heart.

A Movement of the Heart

Affective prayer completes the stages of growth of ordinary active prayer, building upon formal and mental prayer. In the East they say that one goes from the prayer of the lips, to the prayer of the mind, to the prayer of the heart. We experience affective prayer when the affections or sentiments of the heart predominate in our prayer time. What are these sentiments? They can be any human aspiration or emotion. These would include expressions of what are called the four purposes of prayer: adoration or praise; contrition or sorrow for sin; thanksgiving or gratitude; and supplication or heartfelt petition for our own needs or those of others. An easy way to remember these four purposes is with the acronym ACTS: adoration, contrition, thanksgiving and supplication.

Other sentiments would include prayerful expressions of the theological virtues of faith, hope and charity. For example, we might pray: "Increase our faith!" (Luke 17:5). "Jesus, I trust in you!" "Lord, you know everything; you know that I love you" (John 21:17). Sometimes these virtues reach profound depths of prayer. When a person goes through severe periods of doubt and interior darkness, for example, his only prayer might be, "Lord, I believe even when I do not see!" At other times, if all hope seems lost and he feels that even God has abandoned him, that he is desolate, his only prayer against such despair may be the plea: "Lord Jesus, save me" or "God, help me, for I cannot help myself!" The prayer of Hannah, who later became the mother of the prophet Samuel, is an example of such anguished prayer. Hannah was infertile and so distressed over her condition that when she prayed at the temple the priest Eli thought she was drunk! (1 Samuel 1:9–18).

If we are suffering and without human comfort, we might pray a prayer of resignation such as: "Lord, your will be done!" Job in the Old Testament was well acquainted with this kind of prayer in the midst of his excruciating trials: "The Lord gave, and the Lord has taken away; blessed be the name of the LORD!" (Job 1:21). Joy is a special prayer sentiment expressed in a jubilant "alleluia" at Easter or anytime. What more beautiful example do we have of this sentiment than Our Lady's own Magnificat: "My soul magnifies the Lord, and my spirit rejoices in God my Savior" (Luke 1:46–47).

Affective Prayer, Day by Day

Because affective prayer is spontaneous in character, it allows us to speak to God from the heart. This enables us to be more in touch during prayer with what is going on within us. We recognize more easily those feelings that have remained hidden and those issues that touch us in an unconscious way. In fact, those whose relationship with God has grown very trusting can be quite frank with Him. Remember Saint Teresa of Avila's famous remark to our Lord after she fell into a stream and was soaked? He told her that this is how he treats all his friends. She replied, "No wonder you have so few."

The prayers of Jeremiah the prophet likewise come with an honesty and humble boldness, straight from his heart. One of my favorite lines from his prayers is when he says to the Lord, "You will be in the right, O LORD, when I lay charges against you; but let me put my case to you" (Jeremiah 12:1, NRSV). These words make me think that Jeremiah probably never got an ulcer from holding his worries and anguish tightly inside!

As we can see, affective prayer is not only spontaneous; it's often conversational in form as well. Saint Teresa of Avila once described prayer as nothing but a heart-to-heart conversation with God who loves us. We naturally converse with those we love, so why not with God? We aren't likely to hear God speak to us audibly in response to our words to Him, but we sense things in our hearts at times: for example, God can make us aware of certain things, or a feeling of comfort or consolation may come over us, or a sense of trust that God has heard us out.

Abraham's dialogue with the Lord over the fate of Sodom is one of my favorite examples of conversational prayer (see Genesis 18:22–33). It's nothing but a bargaining session with the Lord, asking Him to spare the sinful city if even a few just people live within it. I can testify, based on personal experience, that this passage is patterned on a true-to-life Middle Eastern business transaction.

During a pilgrimage to the Holy Land, I was walking through Jerusalem when the owner of a religious goods store spotted me going by his shop. I was an easy target with my habit on. He ran out into the street, grabbed my arm and said, "Father, I have something very special for you!" I had no money on me at the time and told him so, but he persisted. He practically dragged me into his shop and showed me what looked like a small chalice.

Hitting it with his finger so that I would hear the quality of the metal, he said, "Father, this is pure silver. For you, seventy-five dollars!" When I reminded him I had no money with me, he said, "Father, sixty dollars!" He kept it up until his final offer to me was two little chalices for five dollars! I think our Lord takes delight when we approach Him with such confidence that we bargain with Him this way, especially in intercessory prayer for our needs and those of others. After all, Jesus spent His earthly life in that Middle Eastern culture.

Over time, affective prayer tends to become shorter and simpler. When we know someone very well, we need fewer words to get our point across. If we persevere in affective prayer and at the same time try to live a true Christian life, we become God's good friends. Many of the examples of prayers cited above show this brevity and simplicity of affective prayer.

When our affective prayer becomes more intense and pervades our daily activities, we find ourselves living more concretely in loving union with God throughout the day. This consciousness of God and His continuous presence as we go about our daily tasks is known as "recollection." We are at the point where we can say, as did the second lady on the retreat at the opening of this chapter, "I talk to God all day long."

• THE IMPORTANCE OF SPIRITUAL READING •

There is a great deal of truth in the old saying, "The pen is mightier than the sword." Some people have conquered and subjugated other people with the sword but in the long run, their conquests have failed because they could not win over the minds and hearts of those whom they had forcibly conquered. Thoughts from the pen of another, however, can win hearts and conquer people so profoundly that their steadfast loyalty is assured for life. Just so, spiritual reading, with its message of truth and love, can conquer souls and help people faithfully live the Christian life.

Spiritual Reading and Conversion

God has often used spiritual literature to inspire people to radically redirect their lives. Saint Ignatius of Loyola, the founder of the Society of Jesus, better known as the Jesuits, provides a remarkable example of this. Ignatius was a soldier in the service of his native Spain, but his military career ended when a cannonball broke one leg and wounded the other during a battle. Sent to his family's castle at Loyola to convalesce, he asked for his favorite reading material, books of romance and chivalry. There were none to be had; apparently, a devout sister-in-law had thrown these out. Two other books were available, however, a life of Christ and a collection of the lives of the saints. He had no attraction to such spiritual topics, but he reluctantly began to read simply to pass the time.

God's grace was at work, though, and as Ignatius read these books, he felt a strong attraction to their content. Finally, his reading led him to ask himself a decisive question: "What if I were to do what Francis did, or Anthony, or any of the other saints?" He firmly resolved to imitate the saints, choosing to love Christ ardently and serve under His kingly banner!

Edith Stein, now known to us as Saint Teresa Benedicta of the Cross, also came to conversion through spiritual reading. Born in 1891 into a Jewish family in the German city of Breslau, Edith abandoned her faith at the age of fourteen. During her university years she was a protégé of the famous philosopher, Edmund Husserl, and earned a doctorate in philosophy in 1916. One of the brightest philosophers of the time, she experienced a growing interest in Catholic teaching and began to study the philosophical thought of Saint Thomas Aquinas.

One night, while staying with friends, she picked a book from their shelf and settled in to read. It turned out to be the autobiography of Saint Teresa of Avila; Edith stayed up all night and finished it. As she closed the book in the morning she said to herself, "That is the truth." She became a Catholic and a Carmelite nun and ultimately died at Auschwitz as a result of religious persecution.

Of course, there are also many unknown and less dramatic conversions of ordinary people inspired by reading Christian books. Many, too, who have fallen away from the Church come back when they read something that rekindled their longing for the faith or corrected misconceptions they had about Catholic teachings. (Archbishop Fulton Sheen often said that if he believed what 90 percent of the people who leave the Catholic Church claimed the Catholic Church actually taught, he would leave too!) Consider, also, the many Catholics who might have left the Church had not God led them to a significant writing that kept them from abandoning the boat of Peter from which Jesus preached and still preaches (Luke 5:3; Matthew 16:15–19).

Spiritual Reading and Daily Christian Living
Spiritual reading can help us grow in our life in Christ in many ways. Let's look at four particular benefits of this practice.

It Strengthens Our Faith
Spiritual reading can help us grasp the truths of the Catholic faith more clearly. "Faith seeks understanding," Saint Anselm said, and we should all work to understand

more fully the truths we initially believed on faith. Clarity about these truths serves as a solid foundation for daily Christian life. Many Catholics today, for example, question the value of regular confession. If they understood the purpose and fruits of this sacrament of God's mercy, though, they would appreciate its importance and practice it often.

The truths of the Catholic Church derive from God's revelation in Sacred Scripture and Sacred Tradition. Reading about them and meditating on them stirs our desire to know, love and serve the Lord in this life and our desire to be happy with Him forever in the next. These are, therefore, sacred teachings. Many of the Fathers of the Church studied and wrote their theology on their knees, so to speak, with a prayerful attitude and reverence for divine truth. In a similar way, do we ever think of our reading the *Catechism of the Catholic Church* as spiritual reading, or is it merely an academic study?

It Nourishes Our Prayer
Spiritual reading is the main source of the food for thought that nourishes prayer. A good book on the magnificent gift of the Holy Eucharist, or on the supreme love seen in the passion of our Lord, or on the virtues of Our Lady and the saints, can sustain and strengthen and inform our prayer. Saint Teresa of Avila recommended that we always have a good spiritual book nearby during meditation. When our own thoughts run dry or our hearts

feel so empty that it seems impossible to speak heart-to-heart, an inspiring thought from a good book can be the spark that ignites a wonderful conversation with the Lord. As Saint Teresa also said, He's more eager to speak with us than we can ever be to speak with Him.

It Teaches Us Principles of Christian Growth

Jesus spent three years forming the apostles in the ways of the Christian life in order that they would be equipped to live it fully. We must learn these same ways because they form the principles of our spiritual life. For those willing to learn, solid spiritual authors can provide a kind of general spiritual direction in such essentials as growing in Christian virtue, overcoming temptation and controlling disordered passions. Classics such as Saint Francis de Sales's *Introduction to the Devout Life*, Thomas à Kempis's *Imitation of Christ* or Jean-Pierre de Caussade's *Abandonment to Divine Providence* give many of these fundamental principles. Also, the works of Saint Teresa of Avila and of Saint John of the Cross present the ways of prayer and spiritual growth more profoundly for anyone eager to accept the challenge.

It Affords Inspiration and Motivation for the Journey

Spiritual reading, furthermore, stirs up our motivation to run the race so as to grasp Jesus, our goal and reward, as He has grasped us (Philippians 3:12–16). This is very important because as Saint Augustine said, the road becomes long when we decide to follow Jesus. Even our best motivation weakens with time and often needs reinforcing. Spiritual reading renews us; it gives us a second wind. We'll find this motivation most readily in reading the lives of the saints. In the saints, Pope John Paul II said, we see the action of the Holy Spirit in a very concrete fashion. They inspire us, stir us and, since we humans are instinctively hero worshipers, we find ourselves wanting to imitate them.

Autobiographies of the saints generally have the greatest impact, since they not only describe the outward actions of the saints but also their inner thoughts and feelings. Saint Augustine's *Confessions* is a classic in this field, still life-changing today for many who identify with his struggles on the road to finding God. *The Story of a Soul* by Saint Thérèse of the Child Jesus, another classic, was written under obedience to her superiors but Thérèse herself asked that it be published. She had an inspiration from God, a premonition that her "little way of spiritual childhood" would help many souls to know and love Him.

Sometimes, those who know a saint personally write his or her biography. This was the case for Saint Athanasius when he wrote the *Life of St. Antony,* a book that became a pattern for many future biographies of saints. Other classic biographies were written by authors who may at most have had a passing acquaintance with the saint or who gathered data from those who knew the saint personally, or who used testimonies about the saint given by witnesses during the saint's canonization process. Saint Bonaventure's and Brother Thomas of Celano's biographies of Saint Francis of Assisi are based primarily on evidence they gathered from those who knew Francis.

No matter what type of spiritual reading we do, it's important that we do enough of it. This takes discipline. Fifteen minutes a day seems like a good target, but many people can't do that. They prefer to get into their spiritual reading for an hour or two, as occasion allows, or listen to spiritual tapes (a great substitute when we don't have time to read), especially while in a car. Regardless of how or when we do it, the point is that we *must* do at least a minimum in order to nourish our souls.

• D I S C E R N I N G   G O D ' S   W I L L •

All faithful Christians want to know how best to serve God and His people; they wonder if what they are doing is pleasing to Him and what His will is for their lives. Discerning God's will isn't always easy, but it's always important. Why? Because anything we do has meaning and value only if it is according to God's will. Jesus' own experience stresses this. He said, on coming into the world, that "I have come to do thy will, O God" (Hebrews 10:7). His nearly last words on the cross were, "It is finished" (John 19:30), a reference to His having fulfilled the will of His heavenly Father by completing His redemptive mission on earth. From beginning to end, doing the will of His heavenly Father was the focus and driving force of every moment of His life.

Simple Steps to Knowing God's Will

We can become more adept at knowing God's will if we follow a few basic guidelines. First, it is essential that we pray daily for the grace to know and do God's will faithfully. Jesus Himself taught us to pray to the Father that "Thy will be done, On earth as it is in heaven" (Matthew 6:10). Saint Paul prayed unceasingly for his Colossian converts to "be filled with the knowledge of God's will in all spiritual wisdom and understanding" so they would "lead lives worthy of the Lord, fully pleasing to him, as you bear fruit in every good work and as you grow in the knowledge of God"(Colossians 1:9-10, NRSV). Ask the Holy Spirit to act in and through you and to keep you from doing anything that would offend Him. Mother Teresa of Calcutta prayed daily that if she did anything that day that was not according to God's will, it would fall apart before her eyes.

Second, keep in mind that God usually does not reveal His complete will to us all at once, especially if we are beginners in the spiritual life. Rather than getting the big picture, we more often get just a piece or two of the puzzle. When the Lord called Saint Francis, for example, the saint asked Him what he was to do. Jesus simply told him to go back to Assisi and it would be told him what he was to do. This was only the first step in a long conversion process.

Once we take the first step, however, God usually reveals His will gradually as we are able to grasp its full meaning. By spiritual enlightenment and lived experience, we become more aware of what God is doing in our lives or what He is asking of us. If we stop to think about it, many of us realize that we understand God's will more clearly now than two years ago, and two years ago we understood it more clearly than two years before that.

When Saint Francis heard Jesus tell him from the cross of San Damiano, "Go and rebuild my Church which as you see is falling into ruin," the saint set about repairing dilapidated chapels with stone and mortar. Later on, the Holy Spirit helped him realize he was called to rebuild faith and love in the hearts of the faithful, the Church as the mystical body of Christ.

Two Aspects of God's Will

Saint Francis de Sales viewed the will of God under two aspects. The first he called God's *signified will,* by which God reveals what to do or what not to do. God makes this known to us through His commandments and prohibitions, His Church's teachings and the duties of our particular state in life. When we follow God's signified will, we say we are "doing" or "fulfilling" His will. This is where proper discernment begins, by doing God's will as far as we know it right here and now.

If we follow God's signified will, we will find that, as the saying goes, we bloom where we're planted. This has important benefits. For one, we won't waste present opportunities because we're looking for some extraordinary mystical experience to show us what God wants of us in the future. By doing God's signified will we learn to appreciate the importance of the small, even seemingly insignificant tasks the Lord sets before us. This prepares us to do the bigger tasks when they come along: "He who is faithful in a very little is faithful also in much" (Luke 16:10).

Further, as we accomplish God's signified will, we are working toward achieving any hidden goal the Lord has in mind. Cardinal John Henry Newman, the famous English convert of the nineteenth century, echoed this truth when he wrote: "God has created me to do Him some definite service...I have my mission—I may never know it in this life, but I shall be told it in the next...I shall do good, I shall do His work...while not intending [as in, realizing] it, if I do but keep His commandments and serve Him in my calling."[1]

We shouldn't fret if we don't have a clear understanding of everything we think God expects of us. If someone gives us directions over the phone to a place we've never been, we'll get there if we follow the directions, even if the landscape is unfamiliar. The Ten Commandments are God's directions. If we follow them, we'll reach our destination (heaven) even if we don't always recognize the landmarks—the changing landscape of events and tasks in our personal lives—we pass along the way.

Finally, doing God's will insofar as we know it is a sign of our love for Him. As this love grows, our purity of heart increases. Jesus says that purity of heart enables us to see God (see Matthew 5:8) in the sense that we recognize His presence and actions in our lives. This gift, a result of our maturing in the Spirit, sharpens our spiritual vision and makes us more capable of recognizing God's will in specific instances.

Saint Francis de Sales also talked about God's *will of good pleasure*. This includes, first, those events and circumstances that God directly intends and brings about by the operation of His divine providence. These situations are not dependent on our own efforts. As the saying goes, "Man proposes, but God disposes." In these situations, we speak of "accepting" God's will. Divine providence springs from God's infinite love and wisdom, by which He directs the course of events for His greater glory and our salvation.

Sometimes we are disappointed or confused by such circumstances until it becomes evident what God really intends. We've all experienced this. We start a project with plan A, but before we know it God is moving us mysteriously into plan B. (As Mother Teresa used to say, if you want to make God laugh, just tell Him your plans.) We must be ready to abandon our own preconceived ideas when they do not correspond to God's. For example, Saint Paul, who certainly had the guidance of the Holy Spirit, tried twice to evangelize certain areas of Asia Minor but the Holy Spirit prevented him. Later on, he received a vision to go to Greece, with the result that the gospel came to Europe. We want to avoid blind stubbornness at these times and acquiesce, instead, to God's will. Doing so will bring many unforeseen blessings.

The will of God's pleasure also includes instances where He permits events to happen that He does not directly intend or want. These would include moral evils such as unjust wars, violence, religious desecration and sexual immorality, all of which are contrary to His signified will. Because God gives us free will, He allows us to use our freedom even to do evil. From this evil, however, God will ultimately draw good: "Where sin increased, grace abounded all the more" (Romans 5:20). This aspect of God's will is called His *permissive will*. Original sin is a leading example of this permissive will of God. God never intended Adam and Eve to sin but He permitted their sin to happen to show us an even greater love, the outpouring of His mercy in the incarnation of His divine Son as Lord and Savior. The events that God permits to happen often bring disturbance, even injustice and suffering, and so we speak of "submitting" to God's will, bearing patiently what God sends.

Guidance

Saint Teresa of Avila put a high priority on wise guidance in discerning God's will for our lives. None of us can see ourselves completely. We are a mystery, even to ourselves, with blind spots due to our ignorance or prejudice or similar shortcomings. A wise guide can easily step back and get a better look at a problem or question that we are too close to. A guide can help us question our motives, keep us from panicking when we are in fear and help us find our way back when we stray. A guide who is open to the light of the Holy Spirit can help us interpret things that might otherwise be baffling.

When Samuel the prophet was a young boy living at the temple of God at Shiloh, he heard the Lord call him. Not recognizing the Lord's voice, he misinterpreted the call. It was the priest, Eli, who finally realized what was happening and gave Samuel the sound advice that if he heard the voice again, he was to say, "Speak, LORD, for your servant is listening" (1 Samuel 3:9, NRSV).

This advice to young Samuel sums up the attitude we should have when seeking God's will. We want to prepare ourselves to hear the Lord when He speaks and then, in humble service, be ready to faithfully carry out His will.

• UNANSWERED PRAYER OR, DID GOD SAY NO? •

Someone once said that if heaven had a complaint department, the biggest complaint would be unanswered prayers. People pray, and pray again and then pray some more, but they never seem to get an answer. Why not?

God certainly hears all prayers, but maybe the answer He gives is one we don't expect. I heard about a girl who prayed for a friend of hers who was quite ill. When the friend died, someone said to the girl that God didn't hear her prayer. The girl replied that God did hear her prayer, but God said "no" because He wanted her friend in heaven.

God does say no to many prayers. We believe with Saint Paul that God does all things for our good when we love Him (Romans 8:28), but we cannot understand His infinite wisdom in these matters, for His ways are far above ours (Isaiah 55:8-9). Saint Augustine suggested three reasons why God sometimes says no to our prayers. Using forms of the Latin word *malum*, which means "bad" or "wrong," he said there are three reasons: *mala*, *malo* and *male*.

Mala means "bad or wrong things." Some people ask God for the wrong things or things that will harm them, especially spiritually. Many approach prayer as if they were submitting a Christmas list to Santa Claus: "Please give me a new car, a vacation in Hawaii and a winning ticket for the lottery this week." Their prayer requests are for material things that would only ensnare them in a worldly spirit to the detriment of their salvation and sanctification. Although God would not be inclined to grant these, He may occasionally give such material blessings in order to win a person's affection and ultimately their conversion.

Given this, are we ever permitted to pray for material things? Yes, as long as they are not evil in themselves and as long as we can add at the end of our prayer, "God, I ask this if it is according to your will," or, "God, you know what is best for me!" It would certainly be better spiritually, however, to broaden our perspective in prayer to include the many genuine and urgent needs of others.

Malo means, literally, "in the wrong." Saint Augustine used this word to indicate someone who prays while living a wrong or sinful lifestyle. Generally, God will not answer such a person's prayer. It is said that God listens to those who listen to Him.

During the October 13, 1917, appearance of Mary at Fatima, for example, Lucia asked our Lady to cure certain people. Our Lady said that some would be cured but not others. These latter first had to amend their lives and ask forgiveness for their sins. Nevertheless, God may fulfill the prayer request of a person living a sinful life so as to draw that person to conversion.

Male literally means "wrongly," to ask in prayer but in the wrong way. What is the right way to pray? Jesus stresses two essential qualities for effective prayer: confidence and perseverance.

The parable of the widow who went before the corrupt judge (Luke 18:1–8) illustrates the importance of confidence or great trust. Time after time, she asked him to hear her case, but in his arrogance he refused. Finally, afraid she would wear him out, he granted her justice.

Saint Thérèse said we receive from God what we expect to receive. Judging from all the unanswered prayers, we might conclude that many do not expect much. Yet our Lord assures us of the power of prayer: "The Father will give you whatever you ask him in my name" (John 15:16, NRSV). But Jesus also commented on how we must pray: "Therefore I tell you, whatever you ask in prayer, believe that you receive it, and you will" (Mark 11:24).

Do we always believe that our prayer will be answered? This is precisely the confidence we need in prayer.

Effective prayer is also persevering. Jesus said, "Ask, and it will be given you; seek, and you will find; knock, and it will be opened to you" (Luke 11:9). This certainly strengthens our confidence to pray. Remember, though, that Jesus did not say, "You need ask only once." Nor did He say, "Seek for five minutes and that will be enough."

Nor did He say, "Knock just three times." Persevering prayer requires that we keep asking, seeking and knocking.

Consider Jesus' parable about the man who has visitors arrive late at night (Luke 11:5-8). He doesn't have any food to offer them, so he goes to his neighbor's house and knocks on his door. The neighbor, already in bed, tells him to go away. But the man persists, and the neighbor gets up and gives him whatever he needs, not out of friendship but because he wants to get some sleep. So keep on knocking. If we get discouraged and give up, our request may simply become another "unanswered" prayer.

• WHEN GOD SAYS YES TO OUR PRAYERS •

I believe that God says yes to our prayers more often than no, although I don't know of any surveys that support my conclusion. When He does say yes, however, He may qualify his reply. He may say "Yes, right now," for example, or "Yes, but you will have to wait a little while," or "Yes, but you are going to have to wait a long time," or "Yes, but you will be surprised."

Let's take a look at these four responses. I'll illustrate the first three by comparing God answering a prayer to a person cooking a meal. Three common ways to cook are with a microwave, a stove or a slow cooker, each of which makes a great symbol for how quickly God may respond.

Cooking Up an Answer?

Microwave cooking is nearly instantaneous: you put the food in, push a few buttons and in practically no time the food is piping hot. Sometimes God, in a manner of speaking, puts our prayer "in the microwave": We just about finish saying the prayer and He answers. I have found that God allows Saint Anthony of Padua to use the "microwave" frequently.

Once, for example, I had to make a number of important phone calls but couldn't find the paper on which I had written the phone numbers. I searched everywhere, through papers and drawers and desks, and was feeling very frustrated. Suddenly I thought, "This requires Saint Anthony's help." I stopped my searching and said an Our Father, Hail Mary and Glory Be in honor of this patron saint of finding lost things. Then I put my hand in my pocket, and lo and behold, there was the missing piece of paper! Saint Anthony had done it again, and at microwave speed. In these cases God says, "Yes, right now" in answer to our prayers, sometimes through the intercession of the saints.

Most people cook their meals on a stove, a method that takes a little time. If a pot of water boils in ten minutes, it will not boil in five; if a turkey roasts in five hours, it won't be done in two. On the stove things have to run their course. When God answers our prayers "on the stove," so to speak, He lets them run their natural course.

If a student is praying on Monday to pass an exam he will take on Thursday, his prayer will not be answered on Tuesday. If a pregnant woman is praying for a successful delivery, her prayer will not be answered until the baby in her womb has developed sufficiently. God answers such a prayer by saying, "Yes, but you will have to wait a little while," as the situation runs its course, like a good meal cooking on the stove.

Sometimes God responds to our prayers by saying, "Yes, but you're going to have to wait a long time." This answer isn't easy to take, but it reminds me of cooking with a slow cooker. You put a stew into the slow cooker at eight o'clock in the morning, and it's still cooking at four o'clock in the afternoon. The juices blend together throughout the day, and you end up with a delicious stew.

The slow cooker symbolizes those prayer requests that are too important—in fact, too precious—to hurry through. God wants to give a savory gift, one that usually has a marvelous grace-filled impact not only for the petitioner but for many others who are affected by this slow-cooker prayer in ways only God could foresee.

Usually these slow-cooking prayers involve significant religious experiences, especially a person's conversion. Saint Francis, for example, prayed for nearly three years before he understood the form of religious life that Jesus wanted him to embrace so that he could be a special instrument in rebuilding the Church.

Saint Monica, another example of the rewards of long-simmering prayer, prayed for years for the conversion of her husband. It was the conversion of her son, the great Saint Augustine, however, for which she is best known. Augustine said that his mother prayed for his conversion for sixteen years. She prayed in church twice a day, morning and evening, and Augustine said that the floor where she knelt in prayer was always wet with her tears. She even asked a bishop to talk to her son, but he told Saint Monica that her son was not ready to listen to anyone. At this, Saint Monica burst into tears, prompting the bishop to say, prophetically, that it would be impossible that the son of so many tears would be lost.

God heard Monica's prayers and saw her tears and said yes, but He made her wait a long time. Her prayers and her example have touched countless people over the centuries who identify with her anguished plea. What a marvelous grace God was preparing all those years "in the slow cooker."

What a Surprise!

Sometimes the answers to our prayers involve an element of surprise, and God gives us much more than we ever thought possible. At other times, He gives us something we really need although we might not have known we did. Since it's not exactly the thing we prayed for, we find ourselves disappointed. Later, however, when we look back, we recognize the hand of God and know that the things that took place were really the answer to our prayer. A poem from an unknown Confederate soldier of the American Civil War captures this sort of surprising yes from God:

> I asked God for strength, that I might achieve....
> I was made weak, that I might learn humbly to obey.
> I asked for health, that I might do greater things....

I was given infirmity, that I might do better things.

I asked for riches, that I might be happy....

I was given poverty, that I might be wise.

I asked for power, that I might have the praise of men....

I was given weakness, that I might feel the need of God.

I asked for all things, that I might enjoy life....

I was given life, that I might enjoy all things.

I got nothing that I asked for, but everything I had hoped for.

Almost despite myself, my unspoken prayers were answered.

I am among all men, most richly blessed.[1]

PART TWO

• THE PRACTICE OF VIRTUE •

• TRIALS AND TEMPTATIONS: USELESS
ANNOYANCES OR USEFUL OPPORTUNITIES? •

Why is God always testing us? Why does life seem to be one trial after another?" One of my high school students asked me these anguished questions many years ago. She was right in her observation that life in this world is a time of trial.

Scripture bears this out: "Has not man a hard service upon earth, and are not his days like the days of a hireling?" (Job 7:1). In fact, from the very beginning of their existence, our first parents were put to the test: "And the LORD God commanded the man, saying, 'You may freely eat of every tree of the garden; but of the tree of the knowledge of good and evil you shall not eat, for in the day that you eat of it you shall die'" (Genesis 2:16-17). Eve knew that the command applied to her as well as to Adam (Genesis 3:2-3).

This warfare becomes even more obvious the moment we begin to strive earnestly for holiness. Sirach says:

My child, when you come to serve the Lord, prepare yourself for testing. Set your heart right and be steadfast, and do not be impetuous in time of calamity. Cling to him and do not depart, so that your last days may be prosperous. Accept whatever befalls you, and in times of humiliation be patient. For gold is tested in the fire, and those found acceptable, in the furnace of humiliation. Trust in him, and he will help you; make your ways straight, and hope in him." (Sirach 2:1-6, NRSV)

The struggle with trials and temptations is much like riding a bicycle. Riding downhill requires almost no effort; once you get started you'll coast along with the pull of gravity. Just so, living a life of sin usually doesn't require a lot of effort—let pride and the passions take over and the rest follows on its own!

Riding on a smooth, level surface requires only minimum effort, just enough peddling to overcome the slight resistance of inertia and keep the bike moving steadily. This is a good symbol for lukewarm Catholics who do only enough to keep their outward affiliation with the Church but don't make any real effort to grow in holiness.

Riding uphill, however, requires a great deal of effort to overcome the downward pull of gravity; the more rugged the path and steep the incline, the more effort is required. This is true for those dedicated Catholics who strive to live their faith ardently, who recognize that the spiritual life involves effort and is, in fact, warfare!

Why These Trials?
Why does God allow trials and temptations? The answer is important because it determines how we look at trials in

our own lives and how effectively we deal with them.

It is essential that we understand that God Himself does not tempt anyone. This would be contrary to His holiness; He cannot lead anyone into sin. Temptations come from our three spiritual enemies: "the lust of the flesh and the lust of the eyes and the pride of life" (1 John 2:16). We call these enemies more simply the *world*, or material things with their attraction of wealth, power and greed; the *flesh*, the powerful attraction to sensual pleasures without regard to God's law and purpose for these pleasures; and the *devil*, or pride, the presumption of self-reliance and egotistical vanity. Our trials and especially our temptations originate from our disordered inclinations and passions that seek their own satisfaction apart from God.

We must conclude, then, that God permits us to be tempted so that our love for Him may be known. He doesn't need to know if we love Him; He already knows that. It is we who need to know if we love Him. Every time that we are tempted, we find ourselves faced with the choice to accept or reject His love. Jesus tells us: "He who has my commandments and keeps them, he it is who loves me" (John 14:21). If you keep His commandments, you are telling the Lord that you love Him. If you disobey His commandments or neglect them, you are rejecting the Lord.

But are temptations really necessary? Should we look

upon them as assets or as liabilities in our spiritual growth?

Actually, God teaches us many things through our temptations. For one thing, facing temptations and trials helps us grow in the virtue of humility. Humility is simply knowing and accepting the truth about ourselves. As God's creatures, we are dependent on Him for both our material and spiritual needs. Jesus says, "Apart from me you can do nothing" (John 15:5); we can do nothing worthy of salvation without the Lord's grace.

Temptations have a way of showing us our weakness as we struggle to overcome the lure of passion. Confronted with our weakness, we learn humility by calling upon the Lord for help. Our realization of our need for God is heightened in our time of struggle.

Furthermore, humility helps to deflate our ego, our inclination to pride, vanity, self-reliance and self-love. This is extremely important. Pride caused Lucifer to defy God's command to worship and serve His divine Son in His human nature. Lucifer's response to God's command was: "I will not serve!" Our first parents also sinned by pride when the devil deceived them into believing that by eating the forbidden fruit they would become as gods (Genesis 3:4-5). Through original sin we have all inherited that desire to be as gods.

This is why God will often humble someone by an oppressive temptation or trial after that person has received some extraordinary grace or accomplished some significant work for the Lord and His Church. Saint Paul, for example, recounts that he received an extraordinary revelation in which he was "caught up into Paradise... and...heard things that cannot be told, which man may not utter." But that he might not become proud over this revelation, he was given "a thorn...in the flesh, a messenger of Satan, to harass me, to keep me from being too elated" (2 Corinthians 12:3-4, 7).

Traditionally this "thorn in the flesh" has been understood as a violent temptation of lust. Three times, Saint Paul asked the Lord to take it away but the Lord would not, telling him that His power is made perfect in weakness (verse 9). The temptation kept him humble!

Temptations and trials also teach us zeal and perseverance in the spiritual life. When things are going fine, our fallen human nature has a tendency to become soft and comfortable. We easily become spiritually negligent and careless. Trials and temptations are like a wake-up call. Fighting against them, we throw off spiritual indifference and apathy, we resist sin and sinful attachments, we become more attentive to God. This produces a greater purification in the soul. As G.K. Chesterton once said, it's good when a Christian gets into a lot of hot water because it keeps him clean!

Finally, temptations and trials aid our growth in virtue and in practices of piety. Early Christians used the Greek word *ascesis* to describe the effort at growing in virtue. *Ascesis* originally meant "the work involved in learning an art or a skill" and was later applied to the formation of athletes and soldiers as they trained for sports and warfare respectively. Their training taught them to struggle, to compete and even to endure significant pain. Christians in the ancient world understood well that the struggle for virtue and piety is a similar type of *ascesis*.

Praying All the Time

I've adapted a traditional story from the early desert fathers to illustrate this point. There was an old abba, or father, who had a reputation for praying all the time. A young man arrived in the desert to begin his ascetical training. He happened to meet this abba and asked him how he learned to pray continuously.

The abba said, "If you understand me correctly, the devil taught me to pray all the time!"

The young man was shocked. "The devil wouldn't want you to pray! Why would he ever teach you to pray always? What do you mean?"

The abba answered: "When I first arrived in the desert, I was overjoyed. This was where I always wanted to be. I had never been in the desert alone overnight, however, and when nightfall came, I was afraid. Were there wild animals or other dangers? In my fear I stayed awake the whole night and prayed. When daybreak came, the fear of the night left me.

"But now another fear came upon me: Where would I get food and drink in the wilderness? So I again began to pray earnestly, asking God to help me find something to eat and water to drink. By the end of the day, I had found some, but then the fear of the darkness returned, and I stayed awake all night to pray for protection. When daylight returned, I faced the fear of finding food again.

"This pattern of praying all day and all night went on for some time. Gradually, however, I became familiar with these needs. I no longer feared the night, and I had learned to find food and drink during the day.

"As these physical trials ended, spiritual assaults began. Temptations and trials of all kinds came upon me day and night, and so I resisted them day and night by praying continuously. Finally, when I felt I could no longer endure these trials, I called out to God in prayer and begged Him to lift these difficulties. When He did, I realized that I was left with the gift of praying all the time!"

We can benefit from trials and temptations, but we shouldn't go out to look for them. There are plenty of them around, and they will eventually find us! Jesus Himself taught us to pray: "Our Father...lead us not into temptation, but deliver us from evil" (Matthew 6:9, 13). We mustn't put ourselves recklessly into occasions of sin or foolishly bring on our own problems. When God permits trials, though, we can draw much good from them if we cooperate with His grace. If you feel you are tested continuously, as that young high school girl remarked, pray for the grace to pass each of these tests of your love for the Lord with flying colors.

• JUDGMENTAL THOUGHTS: DO THEY BOTHER YOU? •

The struggle against judgmental thoughts is one of the most common problems in the spiritual life. How often we find ourselves focused on our neighbor's actions, or listening critically to his speech, or analyzing his motives. The result? A lot of negative conclusions or judgments about whatever he did, or said, or intended. Such judgments often offend the charity in thought that we owe to our neighbor.

A friend of mine had an experience that illustrates how easily we can fall into unkind judgments, even when we are being told not to judge. He was at Mass one Sunday with a friend, and the priest preached a sermon against judging other people. My friend noticed a lady with a big hat in a front pew. As the priest spoke against uncharitable thoughts, my friend could see this woman's hat going in a slightly up and down motion. He interpreted her nods to mean that the church needed to hear this message!

As he walked out of church after Mass, a friend turned to him and said, "Didn't Father give it to them!" As my friend related the incident to me, he said, "The priest was talking about not judging people, but there were judgments going on all over the church: The woman was judging the congregation, I was judging the woman and my friend was judging everybody else!"

Jesus Teaches Us to Avoid Unkind Judgments

Jesus very clearly taught that we must avoid uncharitable and condemnatory judgments: "Judge not, and you will not be judged; condemn not, and you will not be condemned; forgive, and you will be forgiven.... For the measure you give will be the measure you get back" (Luke 6:37–38).

Uncharitable thoughts are often referred to as rash judgments because there is insufficient grounds or evidence on which to base them. For example, someone at work might not have cleaned up after using a common worksite and we hear about it. Later, when we go to use that same worksite and find it a mess, we instantly jump to the conclusion, "He did it again!" Yet there is no evidence that the same person is responsible. Perhaps someone else was negligent. Past experience alone does not justify the conclusion that it had to be that same person. Isn't it true that after such an unfounded judgment we often find out it was not the person we faulted but someone else who was responsible? God lets us see we were judging rashly.

Judgments might also be rash if we are attempting to infer the inner motivations of another person. We must not make snap judgments about why other people do what they do. Only God can read the human heart with its complexity and hidden recesses. Often we are unsure of our own motivations, much less the motivations of someone else. We might attribute a bad motive to someone who might really have had a morally good or at least a morally indifferent one (neither good nor bad). This can happen when someone does something that upsets us or interferes with our own plans: "He did it out of spite... or jealousy!" A judgment would not be rash or sinful, however, if there is sufficient evidence to make such a conclusion, or if the person admits to having a negative motive.

There is also the matter of suspicion when judging behavior. A suspicion is not quite a definitive conclusion about someone or something, as a judgment would be, but a certain initial leaning in that direction. A person may have a reasonable suspicion if it is based on partial evidence. Also, a person may have a reasonable suspicion about someone based on that person's past behavior or addictive tendencies. If possible, a person should follow up on his or her initial suspicion by checking to verify whether or not it was founded on truth. Failure to do so, especially if the person acts solely on this initial assumption, would cause the suspicion to be rash, since it lacks sufficient grounds for action or accusation.

Finally, however, there is a place for judgment of others in the Christian life. Many people with serious responsibilities must make such judgments in order to fulfill their responsibilities properly. For example, parents must judge the moral quality of their children's behavior and, if something is out of order, take appropriate steps to correct their children. Those in our seminaries and religious communities entrusted with the proper formation of young candidates must make appropriate judgments as to whether or not these candidates are suitable for ordination or the perpetual profession of vows. Such judgments are absolutely essential to the well-being of the individual candidates and to the universal mission of the Church.

Why Do We Judge Other People?
In order to correct the human tendency to judge others inappropriately, it can help to identify some of the reasons why people do this. Some do so because they have a poor self-image. This is often the case with people who are perfectionists, who believe that nothing is good or worthwhile unless it is done perfectly by themselves or others. Judging themselves harshly, they tend to look for faults in others as a way to make themselves feel better: "I'm not so bad after all! They don't do things perfectly, either!" The more severely the person puts himself down, the more likely he is to judge another critically. As the old saying goes, misery loves company.

The correction here is simple: The individual has to learn to accept himself more realistically, with his good as well as his bad points, with his strengths and weaknesses, his abilities and limitations. Then, to the degree that he can realistically accept himself, to that degree he can genuinely accept others. If he is too severe in judging his own faults, his neighbor won't stand a chance!

Some people judge others from a competitive spirit: "I've got to be the most outstanding! I've got to look the best of all!" Such people often show a tendency toward envy (sorrow at the good someone else possesses or does) or jealousy (fear that another will surpass their ability or popularity). They reason that if the other guy looks better, then they look worse. The remedy here is to remember, as Saint Francis said, that we really are what we are in the sight of God, and nothing more.

The opinion of other people is often fleeting and unimportant, but the judgment of God has eternal consequences. God does not judge us on a comparative basis but judges each one of us as an individual. I have to learn to be the best person I can be and leave others to do the same for themselves. If I am adequately secure in who I am or what I do, I will not feel threatened by others. I may even be able to rejoice in their good, for that is what true love does (see 1 Corinthians 13:4–7).

Finally, some people condemn in others the wrongs they do not condemn in themselves. When we fail to acknowledge our own faults, we will usually see them clearly in others! For example, if someone is very slow in doing things but refuses to accept this fact about himself, the slowness of others might drive him crazy. Why?

Because his fault is staring back at him when he looks at his neighbor. Many times this leads to a hypocritical attitude of righteous condemnation, like the Pharisees who wanted to stone the woman caught in adultery (John 8:3-11). When Jesus challenged them, "Let him who is without sin among you be the first to throw a stone at her" (verse 7), and then began to write their own sins in the dirt, they all dropped their stones and went away, leaving the woman unharmed.

The remedy for this attitude is to come to an honest self-acceptance that in turn will lead to humility. Humble persons are aware that all their good comes from God, and that without His help they cannot do anything worthy of eternal life (see John 15:5).

The best remedy for all judgmental thoughts is to ponder Jesus' words in the Sermon on the Mount:

> Why do you see the speck that is in your brother's eye, but do not notice the log that is in your own eye? Or how can you say to your brother, "Let me take the speck out of your eye," when there is the log in your own eye? You hypocrite, first take the log out of your own eye, and then you will see clearly to take the speck out of your brother's eye. (Matthew 7:3-5)

Our Lord makes the point that if we strive to overcome our own faults, we will realize how difficult a task this is and how patient we must be with ourselves. This realization should help us be patient with others since we know the difficulty they must be going through struggling against their own faults. Remember, the measure with which you measure will be measured back to you.

• THE POWER OF THE TONGUE IS AWESOME.
BE CAREFUL HOW YOU USE IT! •

Developing the virtue of charitable speech is one of the greatest challenges in the spiritual life. Through our words, we can express love, compassion, kindness, patience, concern and many other aspects of charity to those around us. This assumes, however, that charity is alive and well in our hearts for as Jesus tells us, "Out of the abundance of the heart...the mouth speaks" (Luke 6:45, NRSV). In other words, what's inside will be expressed outwardly in our words and actions.

But charity in speech is by no means a simple task, as Saint James acknowledged: "Anyone who makes no mistakes in speaking is perfect, able to keep the whole body in check with a bridle" (James 3:2, NRSV). He compares the tongue's effect on a person to a small bit in the mouth of a horse that can control it, or a little rudder that can steer a large ship, or a tiny spark that can set a whole forest ablaze.

> And the tongue is a fire. The tongue is an unrighteous world among our members, staining the whole body.... For every kind of beast and bird, of reptile and

sea creature, can be tamed and has been tamed by humankind, but no human being can tame the tongue—a restless evil, full of deadly poison. With it we bless the Lord and Father, and with it we curse men, who are made in the likeness of God. From the same mouth come blessing and cursing....This ought not to be so. (James 3:6–10)

Saint James gives us a lot to ponder. Keep this passage in mind as we focus on what I see as probably the biggest challenge we face in this area, that of detraction or speaking unkindly of others.

Detraction: A Very Contemporary Sin

Detraction is the sin of speaking unnecessarily about the real but hidden or secret faults of others, thereby resulting in injury to their reputation and a decline in respect for them. It differs from the sin of calumny, which is the spreading of false reports deliberately fabricated to injure the good name of another. It also differs from talebearing, which occurs when an individual hears something unfavorable about someone and passes that information to another. This is usually done to create enmity between the two persons concerned. As one can easily recognize, calumny and talebearing add further malice to the sin of detraction: calumny adds a lie and talebearing adds the evil of turning people against one another.

When we sin by detraction, we offend two virtues. First, detraction goes against charity, which commands us to love our neighbor as we love ourselves, and not do to them what we would not want done to ourselves. None of us want our good name or reputation harmed. Second, detraction also offends the virtue of justice because all individuals have a God-given right to a good name as long as they do not forfeit that right, which can happen, as we shall soon see.

Detraction can further offend the virtues of charity and justice through its consequences. For example, it can lead to a loss of influence, especially if the detraction was meant to be a defamation of character. Another negative consequence can be the disruption of peace and harmony among family members or friends, which is all the more evil if the detraction was deliberately meant to destroy these relationships. Finally, detraction may even bring about material harm, such as the loss of a job or business transactions the person previously enjoyed.

I have never read a study on the matter, but it seems that people today engage more freely in detraction. Some people mistakenly believe that if the facts they share are true, then they are free to tell others. But this is not correct since individuals still have a right to their good name. If we bring into the open the wrongs that others have done, even years ago but long since repented of, how could those people ever have a chance to change their lives for the better? Their past would always prevent them from getting their present and their future in order. That would be like God holding up our past sins, for which we have repented, as if He had never forgiven them.

Also, these days we see so much detraction in our daily media. For example, many people avidly read tabloid newspapers that print one story after another of uncovered scandal. Witness the many smear campaigns we see in politics where opponents engage in mudslinging, revealing secrets from otherwise confidential files simply to destroy the opponent's reputation.

Christian morality recognizes that everyone has a right to a good name as long as he can retain it. Yet we must ask: Is it ever permitted to reveal the secret faults of another? Yes, because people can and do forfeit their reputation. Consider, for example, the case of public misconduct when officials are caught in wrongdoing. Since the wrong is publicly known or will easily become known, it is not detraction to speak about it. Secret faults may also be revealed in order to protect the good of society, such as, for example, when a candidate running for public office is secretly a member of the racist Ku Klux Klan.

We are also justified in speaking of another's faults in order to prevent physical, moral or spiritual harm to innocent people. For example, a person may warn parents that their child has a friend who spreads pornographic material among other young people. In such a case, there is no desire to destroy the good name of someone else but only the intention of protecting others from spiritual harm. Not only is speaking of the hidden faults of another not sinful in cases like this; it can actually be praiseworthy and downright urgent and necessary.

The Golden Rule

Charity in speech, then, demands that we respect the reputation of others by the way we speak about them, just as we want others to respect our own good name in spite of any of our past hidden wrongs. As our Lord taught in the golden rule of fraternal charity, "do to others as you would have them do to you" (Matthew 7:12, NRSV). If we learn about the past wrongdoings of others who have tried to reform their lives and now present no danger to anyone else, it would be wrong to unjustifiably reveal those faults. If we offend the good name of others without justification, or cause them material loss or broken relationships with family or friends, we have an obligation to make restitution as far as possible for the harm we have done.

We can get a fairly accurate measure of our spiritual progress by examining our speech. The more we speak well of our brothers and sisters, the closer we will come to the God-man who said, "This I command you, to love one another" (John 15:17).

When I was a high school seminarian, every student had to give a talk on our Blessed Lady during the month of May. One of the seminarians shared a thought I have never forgotten. It dealt with receiving Holy Communion which, at the time, Catholics only received directly on the tongue. He said, "Every time you put out your tongue to receive Jesus in Holy Communion, think of it as a doormat which will greet the Lord. He will know whether that doormat says 'welcome' or 'unwelcome' by the way you have used your tongue to speak about others."

• "I Heard It Through the Grapevine." Are We Guilty of Gossip? •

*G*ossip usually refers to the more common types of uncharitable speech. It is generally light talk or idle chatter and newsmongering about the affairs of others. It goes on with friends over a leisurely cup of coffee, or with neighbors over the back fence or with coworkers in the office. This is usually not malicious in nature but rather a simple sharing of the latest newsy tidbits. However, it is still wrong if it offends our neighbor.

Gossiping can result in many of the bad effects of detraction, but usually not to the same degree of harm. If we really want to grow in holiness, however, we must work against this fault. What seems like harmless sharing often becomes exaggerated as the story goes from the lips of one person to the ears of another along the proverbial grapevine.

Let me share an example of how even a simple fact can be blown out of proportion as it travels from one person to another. When I was a young friar in college, I had an accident that injured my heel and required several stitches. I had to use crutches to keep the weight off my foot, and I had to elevate my foot whenever I sat down.

The day after the accident, two busloads of parishioners from my home parish came to the seminary grounds for Mass and a picnic. My parents were unable to come, but many parishioners there knew my family and me. They saw me with my foot elevated as I sat at Mass, and they saw me walking with the crutches around the seminary grounds.

The parishioners left in the late afternoon, and I thought no more of the situation. A few hours later I received a panicked call from my family. My mother was nearly hysterical. When the people had returned home, they had begun calling other parishioners and friends of my family. My condition had worsened with every call. Finally, people who had not been on the bus but who had heard the gossip called my family. One said, "I heard that your son had his leg in a cast!" Another said, "I heard that your son had his leg amputated!" And, finally, someone called and said, "I heard that your son died!" My mother, who had of course become more upset with each phone call, said, "No one called me from the seminary to say anything!" The person who reported my death replied, "They forgot to call you."

Think of all the unintended harm that gossiping does, especially when exaggerations and distortions of the facts happen so easily and innocently. People who start the gossip always do so from their own personal viewpoint. But how accurate, fair and impartial is that viewpoint? Just as beauty is in the eyes of the beholder, so are negativity and distortion. One person might find something quite distasteful and gossip about it in a complaining manner, but someone else might not have a problem with it at all.

In other words, in gossiping we can pick up a lot of unnecessary difficulties that are really someone else's problems. Someone once said, "Believe nothing of what you hear, and only half of what you see, and you will probably have a clearer picture of the truth!" This is helpful advice when it comes to gossip.

If you have a tendency to gossip, here are a few practical steps that will help you overcome the problem. First, remember that the grapevine is like a chain—break one link, and there will be a major disruption. So turn in your membership card for the gossip clique. Second, show no interest in the gossip. Gossipers get a great deal of satisfaction when others get excited over their newsy tidbits. If you disappoint them by showing no interest, they will eventually leave you alone.

Third, resist the temptation to gossip, especially when you have some hot exciting news to share. It can do more for your spiritual growth than wearing a hair shirt for six months.

Fourth, change the focus of the conversation subtly or, if necessary, abruptly. As an old saying puts it, "Great minds speak about ideas; average minds speak about events; little minds speak about people."

Over the years, I have come across a couple of proverbs that contain a lot of wisdom on this topic. "Into a closed mouth, a fly cannot enter." Silence can be golden for many reasons! According to another proverb, "Someone who gossips *with* you will end up gossiping *about* you." If you do not get onto the speaking end of the gossip grapevine, it is less likely you will be on the receiving end. People will respect you more, especially if you learn to keep secrets to yourself. You earn their trust.

If nothing else works, try the remedy one of the saints used when hearing the confession of a woman who was the town gossip. After she confessed so many instances of gossiping, the saint wanted to impress on her that what she considered insignificant chatter was really having far-reaching negative effects. He told her that for her penance, she had to take a pillow filled with feathers, go to the town square, open up the pillow and throw the feathers to the four winds. Then she had to go around and pick up all the feathers.

"Well, that is impossible," the woman complained. "The wind will carry those feathers all over the town!"

"And that is exactly what happens to your gossip," the saint replied. "What you think you are spreading to just one individual soon will spread all over town!"

Needless to say, the penance broke the woman of her habit of gossiping. I have a feeling that remedy would work all the time!

- BUILDING THE CIVILIZATION OF LOVE
  BY OUR DEEDS OF CHARITY •

One of the greatest challenges facing Christians today is the task of building what Pope John Paul II called "the civilization of love." He spoke of this often as a central task of the Third Millennium (for example, see *Tertio Millennio Adveniente*, 52).

Building the civilization of love involves, among other things, a great spiritual struggle in three areas. First, we must counter the crisis of civilization caused by the secularism of our time. As a society we have achieved a high degree of technological accomplishment but we are impoverished by our tendency to keep God at a distance or to forget Him entirely. We need to counter this secularism by the practice of faith, which moves us to believe in God and in all that He has revealed to us and continues to teach us through His Church.

Second, we must struggle against modern man's addiction to greed and lust. Many people today are virtually enslaved by these vices. Living by the virtue of hope, on the other hand, we remember that we are only pilgrims and strangers passing through this world and that our hearts were made for the eternal joys of the kingdom of heaven that have been promised to us.

Third, we must counter the terrible culture of death and its contempt for human life, the precious gift God has given to us. The obvious manifestations of this necrophilia, or love of death, are contraception, abortion, euthanasia and violence. Its other manifestations include the sufferings of poverty, injustice, neglect and exploitation. In short, the human person, created with dignity by God, has become dehumanized. Selfishness characterizes the behavior of many in our post-Christian society. To counter this moral and spiritual darkness, we must bring to the world the light of Jesus and the gospel values. In doing this we build up the civilization of love. Failure to do this simply allows evil to spread. As the Irish philosopher Edmund Burke observed, all that is needed for evil to triumph is for good people to do nothing.

Charity: the Foundation of the Civilization of Love
Our approach to this challenge must be Saint Paul's: "Do not be overcome by evil, but overcome evil with good" (Romans 12:21). In this task, we must cooperate with the grace of the Holy Spirit and exercise faith, hope, truth, justice and solidarity. Above all, though, this work requires love. It begins with God's love for us and ours for Him, and extends to the love of all our brothers and sisters in Christ, even to the very least of them. Jesus has given us His commandment to be our

way of life and guide to action: "Love one another as I have loved you" (John 15:12).

This love begins in the heart—in our thoughts—and is usually expressed initially in our words. But it must not stop there; it must be lived out in our actions. Some of the New Testament writers make this point emphatically. Saint James, for instance, writes: "If a brother or sister is ill-clad and in lack of daily food, and one of you says to them, 'Go in peace, be warmed and filled,' without giving them the things needed for the body, what does it profit?" (James 2:15–16).

Saint John the Beloved Apostle emphasizes the same point: "How does God's love abide in anyone who has the world's goods and sees a brother or sister in need and yet refuses help? Little children, let us love, not in word or speech, but in truth and action" (1 John 3:17–18, NRSV).

What Was Jesus' Love Like?
In order to love as Jesus has loved us, we need to know the elements of His love. Let's reflect on some of its qualities.

A Love of Service
The Lord said of Himself on various occasions, "The Son of man came not to be served but to serve… (Matthew 20:28; see also Mark 10:45). He dramatized this serving love powerfully at the Last Supper when He washed the feet of His apostles. This task was considered so menial that even slaves in Israel could not be compelled to carry

it out. That was why Peter at first resisted letting Jesus do this for him. After finishing the task, Jesus addressed His twelve with the reason for His action: "Do you know what I have done to you? You call me Teacher and Lord; and you are right, for so I am. If I then, your Lord and Teacher, have washed your feet, you also ought to wash one another's feet. For I have given you an example, that you also should do as I have done to you" (John 13:12–15).

In the light of Jesus' words and deeds, we should ask ourselves: Is my love a serving love? Am I prepared in mind and heart to reach out to assist with the true needs of my brothers and sisters in Christ? Or do I usually respond with one of the oldest excuses around: "Am I my brother's [or sister's] keeper?" (Genesis 4:9). If my love is a serving love like Jesus', then I am ready to build the civilization of love.

A Love of Sacrifice

Jesus' love was also a sacrificing love. Sacrifice involves giving and the more we love, the more we are willing to give. Jesus was willing to give all, even His very life: "For the Son of Man...came...to give his life as a ransom for many" (Mark 10:45). Elsewhere, Jesus says that like the Good Shepherd He is, He willingly lays down His life for His sheep (John 10:11, 17–18). As Saint Thérèse of Lisieux said, sacrifice is the food of real love.

The more we give of ourselves, the more we grow in love. Mother Teresa of Calcutta, whose life was one of constant sacrificial love for Jesus hidden in the "distress-ing disguise of the poorest of the poor," said that when we make our sacrifices, it must hurt. In other words, it must cost us something—our time, talents, possessions and especially, our comfort. A spirit of laziness and love of leisure always undermine a sense of sacrifice and dedica-tion. The Venerable Father Solanus Casey, a Capuchin Franciscan, used to say that he looked on his whole life as one of giving, and he wanted to give until there was noth-ing left to give. That should be our attitude. What a differ-ent world this would be if more of us, each in our own state in life and personal circumstances, had a more sacri-ficing love!

The unselfish charity of the early Christians in the Roman Empire impressed the morally corrupt pagans, prompting them to remark, "See how these Christians love one another!" Those Christians were gradually transforming a decadent pagan empire into the begin-nings of a civilization of love. Closer to our own times, Saint Maximilian Mary Kolbe, a Conventual Franciscan, made the supreme sacrificial act of love when he literally gave his life for a fellow prisoner whom the Nazis sen-tenced to die in a starvation bunker. So remarkable was this heroic act of love that even the cruel commandant of the infamous concentration camp at Auschwitz remarked that he had never seen anything like this in that place. Father Kolbe was truly a martyr of love.

A Love of Compassion

Jesus' love was also marked by compassion. To have compassion is to experience what another person is experiencing, to feel his or her pain and suffering and to be moved to do what you can to alleviate it. Compassionate love leads to a feeling of pity which prompts us to acts of mercy.

Jesus teaches us this quality in the beautiful parable of the Good Samaritan.

> A man was going down from Jerusalem to Jericho, and he fell among robbers, who stripped him and beat him, and departed, leaving him half dead. Now by chance a priest was going down that road; and when he saw him he passed by on the other side. So likewise a Levite, when he came to the place and saw him, passed by on the other side. But a Samaritan, as he journeyed, came to where he was; and when he saw him, he had compassion, and went to him and bound up his wounds, pouring on oil and wine; then he set him on his own beast and brought him to an inn, and took care of him. And the next day he took out two denarii and gave them to the innkeeper, saying, "Take care of him; and whatever more you spend, I will repay you when I come back." (Luke 10:30–35)

From earliest times, Christians recognized that Jesus was, in a spiritual sense, this Good Samaritan. God had pity on us after the devastation of original sin, along with our personal sins, robbed us of our right to inherit the kingdom of heaven. In His mercy, He brought us to salvation.

What Jesus has done for us is the pattern of what we must do for one another. By compassionate love we, like Jesus, will be moved to perform works of mercy for those in need. What transforming power they have! Mother Teresa, for example, often told the story of a man she literally picked up from the streets of Calcutta and brought to the Home for Dying Destitutes. His body was covered with maggots and was full of disease. He only lived for two hours more, but they were the greatest two hours of his life. He told Mother Teresa that he had lived all his life in the streets like an animal, but he died in the home like an angel.

Finally, compassionate love, shown in kind deeds of mercy, can speak a language of its own when no other communication is possible. Saint Peter Claver, the great Jesuit missionary to Colombia in South America, provides a very moving example of this. He worked tirelessly among the slaves brought there from Africa who were condemned to live in terrible circumstances. Here is part of a letter by the saintly missionary showing what compassionate love can do:

> There were two [slaves], nearer death than life, already cold, whose pulse could scarcely be detected. With the help of a tile we pulled some live coals together and placed them in the middle near the dying men. Into this fire we tossed aromatics. Of these we had two wallets

full, and we used them all up on this occasion. Then, using our own cloaks, for they had nothing of this sort, and to ask the owners for others would have been a waste of words, we provided for them a smoke treatment, by which they seemed to recover their warmth and the breath of life. The joy in their eyes as they looked at us was something to see.[1]

Inspired by these examples of love, let us set about doing what we can through deeds of service, sacrifice and compassion, thereby building the civilization of love as Jesus asks.

• SUFFERING AND THE LIFE OF VIRTUE •

• JESUS OFFERED HIMSELF FOR US •

If we are to grow in a life of virtue, we must come to terms with the meaning of suffering and the role suffering plays in our lives. There is no better place to start than with Jesus, the Lamb of God, who offered Himself for us so that, forgiven of our sins, we might live forever with God in heaven.

The book of Revelation frequently refers to Jesus as *the Lamb,* calling Him, for example, the Lamb who was slain, the Lamb who is in glory and the Lamb who opens the seals of the Book of Life (Revelation 5:12-13; 6:1, 3, 5, 7, 9, 12; 8:1). In the Gospels, however, there is only one reference to Jesus as the Lamb of God, and that is found in the Gospel of John. John the Baptist baptized Jesus in the Jordan River and the next day saw Him walking toward him. John said, "Behold, the Lamb of God, who takes away the sin of the world!" (John 1:29). To understand what John is getting at here, we must go back to the Old Testament.

Abraham and Isaac: God Supplies the Sacrifice

In the book of Genesis, we read that God put Abraham to the test by telling him to offer his beloved son Isaac as a sacrifice. Abraham was an old man when this son was conceived; up to that time, his wife Sarah had borne no children. But one day, when Abraham and Sarah were "advanced in age," a stranger—the Lord—came by their tent with two companions and the couple offered them hospitality. On leaving, the stranger said, "I will surely return to you in the spring, and Sarah your wife shall have a son." Upon hearing this, Sarah laughed because they were both so old. But this child was a child of promise, and when he was born the next year, they named him Isaac, which means "he laughs" (see Genesis 17–18; 21).

Through this child, God would fulfill all the promises He had made to Abraham including establishing His covenant with Isaac and making His descendants as numerous as the stars in the sky and the sands of the seashore (Genesis 17:21; 22:17). Yet mysteriously, God instructs Abraham to take this son on whom every promise rests and sacrifice him as a "burnt offering" (22:2). The Letter to the Hebrews tells us that Abraham, our father in faith, had such trust in God that "he considered that God was able to raise men even from the dead" (Hebrews 11:19). He was ready, therefore, to obey, and taking wood for the burnt offering and a knife to slay his son, he prepared to carry out the sacrifice. Suddenly, an angel stopped him, saying: "Do not lay your hand on the lad or do anything to him; for now I know that you fear God, seeing that you have not withheld your son, your only son, from me" (Genesis 22:12).

Prior to this, as they were going to the place of sacrifice, an interesting scene unfolds. Isaac, carrying the wood for the offering, prefigures Jesus carrying the cross. He says, "Father!...The fire and the wood are here, but where is the lamb for a burnt offering?" Abraham answers prophetically, "God himself will provide the lamb" (Genesis 22:7–8, NRSV).

Scripture tells us that God did not spare His own Son but He spared Abraham's son because, ultimately, *Jesus* was to be the Lamb.

The Lamb of Sacrifice

In Old Testament times the lamb was an animal of sacrifice, a victim, offered to atone for sin. The lamb bore the sins of those making the sacrifice, and by the shedding of its blood, penitents obtained God's forgiveness. In this regard, Scripture mentions the lamb twice in the Old Testament in a particularly important way. In a passage the Church applies to Jesus, Isaiah the prophet says of the suffering servant of God that he was "like a lamb that is led to the slaughter" (53:7) for He was struck for our sins and bruised for our offenses.

The other significant reference to the lamb in the Old Testament is the story of the paschal lamb that the Jews killed and ate "staff in your hand...and...in haste" (Exodus 12:11) as they prepared to leave the slavery of Egypt. God told the people through Moses that each family was to take a one-year-old unblemished male lamb, sacrifice and eat it and put some of its blood on the doorpost of their homes. That night, when the angel of death passed through Egypt, any home protected by the blood of the lamb was spared. Just so, the blood of Christ spares us; Jesus is that new Paschal Lamb.

I find it interesting that in the Gospel of John, the declaration that Jesus is the Lamb of God follows Jesus' baptism so closely. Recall that the baptism of John was meant for sinners; it was a sign of conversion. John knew that Jesus was innocent. In fact, in the Gospel of Matthew, John wants to prevent Jesus from being baptized and says, "I need to be baptized by you, and do you come to me?" (Matthew 3:14). Jesus told him to let it be.

And Jesus went down into that water that, in a sense, was polluted with the sins of all the people who had been baptized before Him. But going down into those waters, Jesus drew those sins—and all sins, including our own—to Himself. In doing so he made the waters clean.

This is why, later, he gave his own sacrament of baptism the power to take away sin. Interestingly, even today priests and deacons who baptize with water from the Jordan do not bless it. Christ blessed it by His baptism two thousand years ago. In a sense, we see that Jesus took our sins upon Himself by undergoing a ceremony meant for sinners. If He was going to be the victim for our sins, He had to be identified with our sins and that happened at

His baptism. He drew our sins to Himself in the water and took them to the cross as the Lamb of God.

Calvary

As we consider the fact of suffering, it is essential that we consider Jesus' own example. He said, "I lay down my life in order to take it up again. No one takes it from me, but I lay it down of my own accord. I have power to lay it down, and I have power to take it up again. I have received this command from my Father" (John 10:17–18, NRSV). Jesus was willing to endure suffering; He came to be the victim as well as the priest for our salvation.

We must learn to keep in mind Jesus' suffering, freely embraced for our sins, when we are at Mass. Jesus spiritually offers Himself again to the Father in the Eucharist even though He cannot suffer anymore. He is in glory in heaven but in the Mass He offers the Father the love that He poured out on the cross for us, and He pleads with the Father to "forgive them; for they do not know what they are doing" (Luke 23:34, NRSV).

Padre Pio used to encourage Catholics attending Mass to picture themselves standing at the foot of the cross next to the Blessed Mother and Saint John the Beloved Apostle and Saint Mary Magdalene. In truth, during the Mass we are at the foot of the cross in spirit.

Since we commemorate the suffering of Christ every day in the Eucharist, it is fitting that we offer our sufferings to Jesus there. When we unite our sufferings with

His, they become part of the redemptive sacrifice offered for us, our families, our loved ones and the world.

Scripture tells us that as Jesus made His way to Calvary, the soldiers seized a man named Simon of Cyrene and forced him to carry the cross with our Lord (Luke 23:26). Simon was an innocent bystander, just coming in from the country. Don't you think he was angry? Maybe he started cursing and became resentful saying, "Why me? I didn't do anything. Why should I be carrying this cross?" Isn't this just like so many of us when a cross comes our way? Our first reaction is anger. I think that Simon probably was angry but by the time he reached the top of Calvary, he was a different man. He realized he was carrying the cross with Jesus who went ahead of him.

As you, too, carry the cross with the Lord, you will begin to understand the same thing. Jesus is the Lamb, He was our victim, and in a sense, we give our lives back to Him by sharing in His cross. As we do, we come to appreciate what Saint Paul meant when he said: "[W]e proclaim Christ crucified...Christ the power of God and the wisdom of God" (1 Corinthians 1:23-24, NRSV).

C H A P T E R   S I X T E E N

• DID GOD ALWAYS INTEND FOR US TO SUFFER? •

Many people wonder if God always intended for us to suffer. In other words, would we always have had the cross? Would that always have been part of our human experience? How did suffering come about? These questions arise especially when suffering or evil of some kind comes into a person's life. When that happens, many people get angry at God or give up on Him; they stay away from church and even deny God's existence. When tragedies such as the Asian tsunami of 2004 take place, many people asked, "Could there be a God who would allow this to happen?"

We have to deal with this question because the problem of evil, as the philosophers call it, touches all our lives. Why does evil exist? I remember hearing the story of someone who remained a lifelong atheist because when he was a young man he saw another person who had been run over by a truck writhing on the ground in pain, dying. He looked up to the sky and angrily asked God why He didn't do something! That's the problem of evil and because of it, many people do not believe in God. But suffering can also have the opposite effect, drawing us to

God as it forces us to think about questions we would otherwise avoid.

Original Sin

Actually, suffering did not originate with God and was not part of His plan. Suffering traces back to our first parents through the first sin, original sin. Although many people deny or at least doubt the reality of original sin, it is real; furthermore, as the Council of Trent stated, it is in each of us in a personal way.

G.K. Chesterton used to say that you can deny that pouring water on somebody's head in baptism is going to do them any good in terms of solving their problems and those of the world, but you cannot deny that the world has a lot of problems and all of us have our share of them. If you don't believe in original sin, just watch the news on TV and you will be convinced that something is wrong with the world. It doesn't operate the way it should. That is the effect of original sin.

God created our first parents to live in harmony with Him. They spoke familiarly to Him, enjoying a personal level of friendship and love with God. They were also at peace with each other—they felt no shame, disharmony or disordered passion in each other's presence, despite their nakedness—and they were also in perfect harmony with nature around them.

Certain saints throughout history related to nature in a similarly harmonious way. The stories of Saint Francis and the animals, for example, are legendary. He saw all creatures as reflecting God's love and care. For example, he loved lambs because they reminded him of Jesus, the Lamb of God. The doves reminded him of the innocence of God; the innocence of his own great holiness allowed Saint Francis to communicate with these creatures.

Before the Fall, Adam and Eve also enjoyed many freedoms that we do not. They were free from ignorance. Adam, for example, could name all the animals because he understood the nature of each one. Adam and Eve were free from suffering, experiencing neither pain nor sickness, and they were free from death. They were immortal both in body and soul.

A Capacity for God

Saint Bernard of Clairvaux had wonderful insight into the pre-Fall state of our first parents. He noted that they were made in the image and likeness of God. He said that this image is in all of us because God created us with intelligence and free will. By our intelligence we can know God and others in a personal way. To complement our intelligence, the gift of free will enables us to choose to love God and also to love others and even ourselves properly.

Saint Bernard called our ability to know and love God *capax Dei,* a capacity for God. So we say that we are made in the image of God because we have intelligence and free will. As a result, we can know God as God knows us, and we can love God as God loves us. The other creatures in the world around us cannot do that. They love and honor God according to their nature by just being what they are. But we humans, through the "image" of intelligence and free will, can do so in a personal way.

Saint Bernard also explained our "likeness" to God. This likeness consisted in the special freedoms our first parents enjoyed—freedom from ignorance, concupiscence, suffering and death—which made humanity like God. In the imagery of Genesis, our first parents kept and maintained these freedoms because they had access to the Tree of Life. Our first parents lost these freedoms for themselves and for us as their descendants when, in the Fall, they sinned through pride and disobedience. God had warned them not to eat of the tree of the knowledge of good and evil, for if they did, they would die (Genesis 2:17).

Saint Bernard said that after original sin we have kept the image of God since we still have knowledge and love. Now, however, these are imperfect. Our knowledge, distorted by original sin, is clouded by ignorance; we even question God and His laws and ways. Original sin has also distorted our love. Saint Thomas Aquinas writes about the wound of malice in the will; this means that although we can love God, we don't always choose what is right. Many distorted aspects of self-love lead us to rebel against God. So Saint Bernard taught that we kept the *image* of God but lost the *likeness* to Him. As a result of losing our freedoms, he says we were exiled into a land of "unlikeness." This is the world situation as we have it now. It is not the original likeness to God that God intended.

In the Land of Unlikeness

Saint Paul says that in Adam we all sinned (Romans 5:19). Somehow we share in the responsibility for the Fall; although I can't explain this shared responsibility, I know that every day I experience the effects of original sin in myself. Saint Bernard said that when we were exiled into this land of unlikeness, we could not find our way back to the land of likeness. Will we ever get back there? How will the freedoms we lost be restored to us so that we can get back our likeness to God?

Of ourselves, we were hopeless and helpless. But immediately after Adam and Eve sinned, God promised a redeemer. He said to the serpent, the devil, who had deceived Adam and Eve: "I will put enmity between you and the woman, and between your offspring and hers; he will strike your head, and you will strike his heel" (Genesis 3:15, NRSV). God promised a savior who would defeat Satan and save His people.

By becoming man, Jesus came to our land of unlikeness, but not in the glory or power that were His as the Son of God. He came in humility, obedience and poverty because our sin was a sin of pride and disobedience. Therefore, He would redeem us in the opposite way: by humility to counter our pride, by obedience to counter our disobedience, by poverty to counter our spiritual avarice to want to be gods! In this way, He would show us how to return to the Father. That is why Saint Paul wrote that Jesus came "in the likeness of sinful flesh" (Romans 8:3). He didn't come like Adam before the Fall because Adam before the Fall could not suffer; He came like Adam after the Fall and so He was like us in every way but sin.

Since all suffering traces its way back to that original sin, God would use suffering to redeem us. He used the sufferings of His Son to pay the price for our sins, and He joins our own personal sufferings to those of Jesus to redeem each one of us. By following Jesus in suffering, in humility and in obedience in this world, we will come to the likeness of Jesus in glory in the kingdom of heaven.

Suffering and Personal Sin

We can go a little further and ask, "Is suffering related to our own personal sins? Do the personal sins that we commit each day bring suffering upon us?" The answer is not all that clear; Scripture answers with a "yes" and a "no." Remember Job? Job was an innocent man although he probably had his faults since even the just man falls seven times a day (Proverbs 24:16). But he certainly was tested when God allowed Satan to harm him and his family. All his children died, and his sheep and cattle were taken away. But despite his bitter sufferings, Job did not curse God. Then God allowed Satan to harm Job himself, and severe boils erupted all over his body. Still, Job was faithful and responded with trusting surrender to God's will: "The LORD gave, and the LORD has taken away; blessed be the name of the LORD" (Job 1:21). Job had not sinned, yet he suffered. Nevertheless, Scripture offers examples of personal sin bringing punishment upon the people, as when God immediately punished Korah, Dathan and Abiram and their clans when they rebelled against Moses in the desert (Numbers 16:23–33).

In the New Testament, sometimes Jesus Himself related suffering to sin. The Gospel of John recounts the story of the paralyzed man who remained with other persons with various infirmities at the side of a pool that had healing properties. When the water in this pool stirred—thought to be moved by an angel—the first one who entered would be healed. This man, having no one to help him, had been lying there for thirty-eight years. Jesus healed him but gave him a warning: "Sin no more, that nothing worse befall you" (John 5:14). It seems obvious that Jesus related that man's suffering to certain sinful deeds he had done.

On another occasion, some friends carried a paralyzed man to a house where Jesus was (Mark 2:1–12). There was such a crowd that they couldn't get near him, so they hoisted the man up on the roof, pulled off the clay tiles, and lowered him down. They were determined to get this man to Jesus who was indeed impressed with their persistence: The Gospel account says that Jesus saw *their* faith—

not *his* faith, the faith of the paralyzed man, as we might expect.

Even though this man's paralysis was obvious, Jesus doesn't say, first thing, "I'm going to heal you." He says, "My son, your sins are forgiven" (Mark 2:5). Jesus finds the man's sins, not his paralysis, the most striking part of this encounter. Why did Jesus have to forgive his sins? The man didn't outwardly acknowledge them although maybe in his heart he did. No doubt he was aware of the wrongs he had done and was sorry for them; Jesus must have read that sorrow in his heart, and He forgave him. Could those unforgiven sins have been an obstacle to his healing? Maybe, and maybe they were also the cause of his suffering.

When Jesus forgives the man, the scribes condemn Him in their thoughts, accusing Him of blasphemy since only God can forgive sins. Jesus read their thoughts and said, "Which is easier, to say to the paralytic, 'Your sins are forgiven,' or to say, 'Rise, take up your pallet and walk'?" (Mark 2:9). Obviously it's easier to say, "Your sins are forgiven" because you can't prove it, only God would know for sure. So Jesus said, "'That you may know that the Son of man has authority on earth to forgive sins'—he said to the paralytic—'I say to you, rise, take up your pallet and go home'" (2:10–11). And the man immediately got up, picked up his mat and walked out. In this case, the Lord seems to connect the sins of this man with his paralysis.

Apart from anything else, common sense tells us that the things we do might bring sad results. Persons who drink to excess or use recreational drugs may later suffer negative effects in their life and health. Infidelity and abortion bring anguish, guilt and shame. Often, people blame God for sufferings they brought on themselves through their own irresponsible behavior. I once read about a young woman who had premarital sex and, when she found out she was pregnant, said rather angrily, "God, why did you allow that to happen?" Blame God. He's an easy target.

Sometimes God does allow us to suffer punishment in this life for our sins. I lived with an old friar who used to say, "God doesn't only pay on weekends." Sufferings do come, at times, to turn us from our sins or to cleanse us of sin's aftereffects such as self-love. It is a little bit of purgatory.

But what about suffering that comes about as a result of an accident or violence? In the Gospel of Luke, some people told Jesus about a situation in which Pilate cruelly killed some Jews and mingled their blood with the sacrifices they were offering. In reply, Jesus brought up an incident in which a tower fell on eighteen people and killed them. He said, "Do you think that these Galileans were worse sinners than all the other Galileans, because they suffered thus? I tell you, No; but unless you repent you will all likewise perish" (Luke 13:2–3). Jesus' point is that suffering that is the result of accidents, natural disasters, human violence and the like, should be seen as a warning to refrain from sin in our own lives.

Finally, although Jesus sometimes clearly relates suffering to personal sin, at other times He clearly does not. The classic example of this is the case of the man born blind. When the disciples see this man, they ask our Lord, "[W]ho sinned, this man or his parents, that he was born blind?" (John 9:2, NRSV). The Pharisees actually taught that a person could sin in the womb; they concluded that those born with infirmities or sickness probably sinned before birth and were now being punished. Or maybe their parents sinned and God punished them with infirmity in their child. Jesus answered, "Neither this man nor his parents sinned; he was born blind so that God's works might be revealed in him" (John 9:3, NRSV).

Mercy

God will use all suffering as He uses all other things, for His honor and glory: "We know that all things work together for good for those who love God" (Romans 8:28, NRSV). Our sufferings are meant to help us understand the glory of God, particularly His mercy. Jesus told Saint Faustina, whom He called His apostle and the secretary of His divine mercy, to copy down everything He told her because He wanted a vast throng, for all eternity, praising Him for His mercy.

One of the reasons God permits suffering and difficulty is precisely so that we might turn to Him and experience this mercy. Saint Francis used to say that before the Fall of Adam and Eve, God gave us everything out of pure love. After the Fall, by which we made ourselves unworthy of that love by sin, God gave us everything out of His mercy. Mercy can be defined as love given to someone undeserving of that love. In heaven, then, we will praise both His love and His mercy for all eternity.

In short, God allows evil so that He might bring about greater good through it. Mother Teresa told me that we are only going to realize when we get to heaven how many graces came to us because of the poor, the needy and the infirm. She said that we can't do anything for God in heaven because He is perfectly happy there. Therefore, He became man. Now we can do something for Him because, as He said, "I was hungry and you gave me food, I was thirsty and you gave me drink" (Matthew 25:35). Jesus also mentions the naked who need to be clothed, the homeless who need shelter and the sick and imprisoned who needed to be visited. We can do good directly to our neighbor in need and indirectly through that neighbor to Jesus Himself, something we would not be able to do if these sufferings did not exist. In the wisdom of God, a greater good came about because of original sin and our personal sins. This wisdom of God can be seen in His mercy.

Preventive Suffering

Two kinds of suffering have relevance to sin in our personal lives: preventive suffering and corrective suffering. Let's look first at preventive suffering. These sufferings happen by God's providence, intended by Him to prevent us from falling into sin. Many of our disappointments in life fall into this category. Maybe we didn't get the job we wanted, or failed to achieve the recognition we hoped for, or didn't marry the person we thought was the spouse of our dreams. So many disappointments come to us in the course of our lifetime, but through it all God's providence is at work. Even though disappointments can be very hard to bear, He is guiding everything by His wisdom, His providence and His love.

When we look back on many of these disappointments, we sometimes can see God's wisdom at work and we end up thanking Him. For example, I was once given a change of assignment that I didn't want. I was very happy where I had been for six years, and this new assignment had a number of problems. Because of my vow of obedience, however, I went to the new situation with some sadness and trepidation. Ironically, within two years the whole scenario reversed itself. Changes occurred in my previous assignment that would have been difficult to handle, while changes occurred where I was transferred that made it a very fulfilling assignment. In my nearsighted judgment I was happy where I was but God, in His farsighted providence, foresaw that I would have become quite unhappy if I had stayed there.

I once worked part-time as a chaplain in a VA hospital. A paraplegic Protestant minister used to go around the hospital in a motorized wheelchair ministering to a number of quadriplegic and paraplegic veterans. He always had a sign on the back of his wheelchair with a thought for the day. The one I remember best is the one that read: "Don't be angry if none of your dreams came true; just be thankful that none of your nightmares came true either." Isn't that good advice? God foresees that certain situations will bring us harm, especially spiritually, and may even endanger our eternal salvation, so He prevents them from happening.

Preventive suffering can occur in innumerable ways. Someone finds himself tied down taking care of an elderly parent, for example, while someone else has children who demand a lot of loving attention and care. On the other hand, some people seem able to go their merry way seemingly without a care in the world. Those who are burdened may envy or resent the carefree, but perhaps they don't appreciate what God is doing. We cannot always see the true value of our efforts and suffering until the final results are in. For example, the harried mother busy with young children will often reap the reward of adult children who love and care for her in her later years.

Once, when I was teaching in a Catholic high school, a priest from another high school came and gave a talk to our students. He told about one girl who came into his class every Monday morning bragging that she had no curfew and could do whatever she wanted over the weekend, including staying out all night. The other students, in contrast, always complained about their strict weekend curfews. One Monday, however, the girl came in crying. The priest asked her, "What's the matter? You're always in here on Monday morning bragging about your freedom on the weekend." She responded: "I realize now that the only reason my parents don't give me a curfew is that they don't care." That is terrible suffering. While the others balked about their curfew, the rules were a type of preventive suffering that showed that mom and dad cared.

Corrective Suffering
Corrective suffering is meant by God to call us back from sin and to draw us closer to Himself. It consists of the trials God allows in order to reawaken a person's faith and love. As the old saying goes, "There are no atheists in foxholes." When people face the ultimate realities and struggles, they begin to think more seriously. God allows hard times for a reason. Saint Francis, for example, was captured after a battle and imprisoned for about a year. Later on, he was sick for six months. Saint Bonaventure tells us in his biography of Saint Francis that adversity prepares us to receive the Holy Spirit. Just so, after all

these sufferings Saint Francis experienced a great conversion in which he received the Holy Spirit.

Many times people come to mature faith only when
they face the ultimate reality about life, namely that we
are not meant for this world alone. Teenagers generally
live with the attitude that they are invincible and immortal. I have noticed that when a teenager dies, the funeral
parlor is jammed with young people. They come *en masse*
because it is incredible to think that one of their own,
someone their age, died. Sometimes God will permit that
to happen because such suffering stirs people, especially
the young, to think about the ultimate direction of their
own lives. Even the good thief only came to this realization as he faced death on his cross.

I often feel uneasy when I hear people say, "Everything
is going fine in my life. I have no problems." In prosperity,
human nature tends to forget God and take His blessings
for granted. It is in adversity, as I have pointed out, that we
turn to Him. It has been said that God and man are on a
kind of seesaw. When man is down, God is up. Churches
are filled in times of difficulty. But when everything is fine,
man is up and God is down and people neglect faith. We
must learn to love God regardless of whether we are in
obvious need of His help or not; we should love Him for
His own sake and not just for our own sake.

The day after the tragedy of September 11, for example, I happened to read a meditation taken from the writ-

ings of Father Walter Ciszek. Father Ciszek, an American Jesuit missionary in Eastern Europe, spent twenty-three years in Soviet prisons and gulags. (His cause for canonization has been opened and he has been named a Servant of God, the first step forward in the process.) He wrote that sometimes people become comfortable in their prosperity, gradually take God's blessings for granted and then begin to forget Him. God may send little trials to turn these people back to Him but sometimes God has to turn their whole world upside down to get their attention. When I read that, I was stunned. I thought to myself: "God just did that! He got our attention yesterday by turning our world upside down." Probably no event in American history in the last sixty years has affected us as much as 9/11, and it will continue to affect us.

Often, sufferings are related to great evil and when great evil exists, it will eventually be destroyed. When reporters asked Pope John Paul II if AIDS was the wrath of God, he said no, it was the mercy of God. He was no doubt referring to certain spiritual effects following upon the AIDS crisis. Many people with AIDS probably turn away from a sinful life because, faced with the possibility of death, they want to give their lives back to God. The possibility of contracting AIDS may dissuade others who were thinking of living a promiscuous sexual life from giving in to such sin. In both instances, AIDS could be used by God either to convert a sinner or to prevent someone from becoming one. That's why Pope John Paul II could say AIDS was the mercy of God because to lose one's soul would be the greatest suffering of all.

Vince Lombardi, the great football coach, used to say, "Winning isn't the main thing, it's the only thing." In the same way, we can say that our salvation isn't the main thing in life; it is the only thing that really matters. After all, Jesus said that if you gain the whole world but lose your soul, what have you gained in the end? Nothing.

God is always calling His people back to Himself, and God can deliver us no matter how far we are from Him. Even in the greatest sufferings and tragedies, God's love, mercy and providence are always at work.

CHAPTER SEVENTEEN

• THE SUFFERING THAT REDEEMS SOULS •

As people progress in the spiritual life, they will experience an increasing desire to work and pray for the salvation of souls. In fact, if they don't experience this, one would almost question whether or not real growth is taking place. Why? Because you cannot love Christ more without loving those for whom He gave His life. Suffering can play a part in this redeeming work.

The Example of Saint Thérèse of Lisieux

In her autobiography, *The Story of a Soul,* Saint Thérèse spoke of her life as being divided into three periods. She called the first period the "joyful mysteries," a time filled with close family love and pleasant memories. This lasted until her mother died when Thérèse was only four-and-a-half years old. She called the second period the "sorrowful mysteries" because, with the death of her mother, Thérèse entered a time of general depression that lasted for ten years. She was very sensitive and easily gave way to tears if hurt.

This period drew to a close after midnight Mass one Christmas when she received what she called her "Christmas miracle." According to the custom for French children, she had left her shoes out to be filled with candy and little gifts. She returned from Mass eager to open these presents.

Her father was annoyed to see her shoes there; he felt that that Thérèse, nearly fourteen, was too old for this. Thérèse headed up the stairs to put her coat away and her father turned to Celine, Thérèse's sister, and said with some irritation, "I hope this is the last year that Thérèse does this." He didn't realize that Thérèse could hear him but Celine, standing at the bottom of the stairs, looked up at her sister and expected to see a flood of tears. But as Thérèse said later, Jesus changed her heart in an instant and she simply walked up to her room, composed herself and went down and joined her family as if nothing had happened.

She revealed later that her depression completely lifted then and there, and that is why she referred to this incident as her Christmas miracle. When she entered Carmel she took the title "of the Child Jesus" in commemoration of this momentous Christmas event. Thérèse referred to the rest of her life after the depression lifted as her "glorious mysteries."

Saint Thérèse said that when this sorrowful period ended she was filled with an enormous desire to save souls for Jesus. One story in this regard stands out. She prayed and had Masses offered for the conversion of a man named Pranzini who was condemned to death for killing three people. His refused to repent and go to confession.

Thérèse asked the Lord to give her a sign that Pranzini repented even if he didn't go to confession. He refused the priest but moments before his execution he reached up, took hold of a nearby crucifix and kissed it. Saint Thérèse took that as her sign that Jesus had received her prayers, her Masses and her sacrifices, for the conversion of this man.

Mother Teresa's Spirituality

Displayed in each convent chapel of the Missionaries of Charity there is always a very large crucifix on the side of which are the words, "I thirst." Mother Teresa of Calcutta focused her spirituality on these words that Jesus spoke as he hung on the cross (John 19:28).

In fact, Mother Teresa's call to holiness centered on her desire to satisfy the thirst of Christ that she saw as both physical and spiritual. Jesus experiences his physical thirst even now in the least of His brothers and sisters. As He says, "I was hungry and you gave me food, I was thirsty and you gave me drink" (Matthew 25:35). The people in turn ask Jesus when they saw him hungry and fed Him, or thirsty and gave Him something to drink. He says in reply, "Truly, I say to you, as you did it to one of the least of these my brethren, you did it to me" (25:40). Mother Teresa carried out her great works of compassion in order to satisfy the thirst of Christ in a physical way through meeting the needs of the poor, the least of His brothers and sisters.

But she also saw Jesus' thirst as a spiritual thirst, a longing to draw souls to Himself. Jesus had said, "I, when I am lifted up from the earth, [on the cross] will draw all men to myself" (John 12:32). We can see this thirst for souls in the following incident. Our Lord was at a well in Samaria when a woman came to draw water; she was one of His lost sheep and He was the Good Shepherd. He said to her, "Give me a drink" (John 4:7), a request that we recognize as related to His thirst on the cross. Although He was physically thirsty, He wasn't interested in the water at the bottom of the well. He was really thirsting for her salvation. Saint Francis of Assisi used to say that nothing should take precedence over the work of the salvation of souls for whom Jesus suffered and died and shed His precious blood. For to love God is also to love one another; and the greatest love we can give to another is to be concerned for that person's eternal salvation.

It came to light after Mother Teresa's death that she felt virtually no spiritual consolation during the fifty years of her ministry to the poorest of the poor. Her spiritual life was utterly dry. You would never have known that if you knew her personally, as I did. Her trial of spiritual darkness caused her great interior anguish, yet she accepted this suffering with complete trust and even a spirit of cheerfulness. She persevered in pure love of God, and many souls were saved.

Our Co-redemptive Mission

Each of us, if we are baptized, has a co-redemptive mission with Christ That means that Jesus is asking us to work with Him for the salvation of the world. Because of our union with Christ, as long as we are in the state of grace we will be bringing souls to God in some way. The more conscious we are of our co-redemptive mission, however, the more souls we will bring to the Lord because we will make a more determined effort. That is one reason why living in the state of grace is so very important.

Saint Paul tells us about our co-redemptive mission in his Letter to the Colossians where he writes: "I rejoice in my sufferings for your sake, and in my flesh I complete what is lacking in Christ's afflictions for the sake of his body, that is, the church" (Colossians 1:24). These words indicate that Jesus wants us to unite our daily sufferings and our struggles to be faithful to Him with His own sufferings that they might have a redemptive quality.

Christ won for us all the graces necessary for the salvation of the whole world. But in order to distribute those graces to individual souls, He asks you and me to work with Him, to pray for these souls, to offer our struggles every day that the graces Christ won may be poured forth upon the souls most in need of them. These are the merits of the life, and especially the sufferings and death, of Christ. It is not that Jesus could not redeem the world by Himself. He could But He wants you and me to share in this beautiful work of bringing souls to Him.

Sacrifices Freely Chosen

There are two kinds of redemptive suffering. The first consists in the things we do spontaneously for the love of Jesus and the conversion of souls. Fasting, for example, falls into this category. Giving up curiosity about situations that are none of our business, for example, can be a form of fasting and a very big penance. Fasting from food is an ancient discipline; Scripture says that fasting united to prayer drives away the demons.

We certainly need that in these days when demonic influence is spreading. It is not only Christians, however, who recognize the value of fasting. Even the enemies of Christ and the Church recognize its power. A friar told me about an encounter he had while on an airplane during the days when airlines served a meal. The lady next to him didn't take a meal and he commented on that. She said that she was fasting and he said, "Oh, that's very good." Then she said, "I am fasting to destroy Christian families." She was involved in the satanic.

It might come as a surprise to realize that there are people in this world who are fasting and doing similar things to destroy Christians, you and me. It is obvious that many in the media are intent on destroying Christian institutions and values. Undoubtedly, Satan inspires much of the evil; it's not simply human evil. He twists the thinking of some of these people, making them determined to destroy our life in Christ. What are we doing to bring them to Christ, to redeem them, to counter their power in the world?

The woman who was fasting was cooperating with Satan in his determination to destroy Christian families. This happened some time ago, and we can be sure that she and others like her are still pursuing this agenda. With some success, too! The issue of gay marriage is pertinent here because it is part of Satan's assault on family life. We cannot be indifferent, brushing this issue aside with an "Oh well, this is what they want to do, why not?" Once society recognizes the "marriage" of two men or two women, a great deal of confusion will follow. Marriage is a sacred institution created by God and intended to be between one man and one woman. This is biologically and psychologically evident in the makeup of men and women, a fact that many people refuse to consider.

Marriage is also a sign of God's covenant with His people. Further, Scripture tells us that "in the beginning" God created us "in his own image...male and female" (Genesis 1:1, 27). "Therefore a man leaves his father and his mother and cleaves to his wife and they become one flesh" (Genesis 2:24). Pope John Paul II's teaching on the theology of the body is extremely pertinent to this issue and should be read by all Christians concerned with a proper understanding of sexuality. We must educate ourselves, speak out, pray and sacrifice for the conversion of souls because if we are silent now, it is going to get worse in the days ahead.

Sufferings Accepted From the Hand of God

Accepting the sufferings and hardships that come our way each day is the second form of redemptive suffering. Suffering will come, even if it consists of being faithful to your vocation in life and your daily duties. You might have to get out of bed at 6:00 AM every day in order to get to work on time. Do you like to do that? I don't think you do! If you call the boss and say, "Hey, I don't feel like coming into work today," he may say, "Well, you know what, you don't have to because I just fired you." We have to be faithful to our tasks despite the effort because we want to be faithful to the commitments we have made to our family or others.

When things go wrong or not to our liking—as when someone disappoints us, criticizes us or irritates us—do we accept it with patience? Do we accept this suffering with patience and even resignation and abandonment to God regarding what He is permitting in our lives? If we do, we learn to trust that this little sacrifice offered to God is like a splinter of the cross that Jesus asks me to carry with Him and for Him. He will unite it to His cross for the redemption of the world. This is why, when we read the lives of the saints, we are amazed at the great sufferings they endured for the salvation of souls.

The Example of Saint Paul

Saint Paul, originally a fierce enemy of the Church, suffered greatly for the cause of Jesus. Prior to his conversion, he had witnessed and approved of the stoning of Stephen, the first martyr of the Church. One of the gates in the wall of the city of Jerusalem is still called Stephen's Gate and is located near the Church of all Nations. It was here that a group of Jewish zealots dragged Stephen out of the city and stoned him to death. As they stoned him, they placed their garments at the feet of a young man by the name of Saul of Tarsus, later to become Saint Paul (Acts 7:51–60).

Saul persecuted the Christians zealously. While he was traveling to Damascus to arrest Christians there and bring them back to Jerusalem for trial, Jesus suddenly appeared to him. He asked: "Saul, Saul, why do you persecute me?" (Acts 9:4). Saul, stunned, fell to the ground and asked: "'Who are you, Lord?' And he said, 'I am Jesus, whom you are persecuting'" (Acts 9:5). The vision left Saul blind for three days. Our Lord then appeared to a man in Damascus named Ananias and told him to go to a house on Straight Street and baptize a man he would find there, Saul of Tarsus.

Ananias told the Lord that he had heard all about the evil this man had inflicted on the Christians in Jerusalem and pointed out that he was here to persecute the believers in Damascus. I've always liked Ananias! Here he is, having a vision, and trying to fill Jesus in just in case our Lord was not up on the latest news about Saul. He might as well have said: "Lord, maybe you haven't heard the latest on this man, but I don't think he's the kind of guy you want to baptize. And maybe he's not the kind of guy I want to get too close to." Jesus said He knew all about that but this is the man He has chosen. Jesus continued: "I will show him how much he must suffer for the sake of my name" (Acts 9:16).

And suffer he did. In the Second Letter to the Corinthians, Saint Paul makes the point, first, that "we have this treasure in earthen vessels, to show that the transcendent power belongs to God and not to us" (2 Corinthians 4:7). This treasure is Christ's grace within us, the power of the Spirit. He then goes on to say:

> We are afflicted in every way, but not crushed; perplexed, but not driven to despair; persecuted, but not forsaken; struck down, but not destroyed; always carrying in the body the death of Jesus, so that the life of Jesus may also be manifested in our bodies. For while we live we are always being given up to death for Jesus' sake, so that the life of Jesus may be manifested in our mortal flesh. (2 Corinthians 4:8–11)

Every day, like Saint Paul, we too carry in ourselves that dying of Christ through our struggles, through our desire to be faithful to Him.

Later in that same letter, Saint Paul elaborates on his sufferings in order to defend himself against competitors in Corinth who were speaking out against him.

> Are they Hebrews? So am I. Are they Israelites? So am I. Are they descendants of Abraham? So am I. Are they servants of Christ? I am a better one—I am talking like a madman—with far greater labors, far more imprisonments, with countless beatings, and often near death. Five times I have received at the hands of the Jews the forty lashes less one. Three times I have been beaten with rods; once I was stoned. Three times I have been shipwrecked; a night and a day I have been adrift at sea; on frequent journeys, in danger from rivers, danger from robbers, danger from my own people, danger from Gentiles, danger in the city, danger in the wilderness, danger at sea, danger from false brethren; in toil and hardship, through many a sleepless night, in hunger and thirst, often without food, in cold and exposure. And, apart from other things, there is the daily pressure upon me of my anxiety for all the churches. Who is weak, and I am not weak? Who is made to fall, and I am not indignant? (2 Corinthians 11:22-29)

This quote reveals the heart of a great saint, one the Lord chose and gave a generous share in His cross. Paul willingly carried that cross because he knew it was to work for the salvation of souls.

Saint John Vianney

When Saint John Marie Vianney, the Curé of Ars, first went to the sleepy village of Ars, people told him he'd have nothing to do there. Nothing ever happened in Ars. By the time he died over forty years later, ten trains a day left Paris carrying all the people who wanted to go to confession to this humble priest. Saint John fasted almost continuously and offered endless sacrifices for the conversion of souls. His life was also filled with trials of all sorts. The devil often tormented him, even shaking his bed and setting it on fire. One assistant remained with him for only a single night. He was so frightened by the devil's attacks on the saintly priest that he never returned!

No one else ever dared to become his assistant, so the Curé carried out his duties alone. When he tried to take a retreat with other diocesan priests, the bishop refused to let him go, telling him that he didn't need a retreat but needed to get back to his people who needed him. They called him "the priest who lived in church" because he sometimes spent the night in the church, praying. When the devil gave him an exceptionally hard time, he would say, "The devil is crazy! He's going to lose another big soul tomorrow." Then some "big fish" would come into the confessional the next day.

Saint John Vianney spent fifteen hours a day hearing confessions. One time a possessed man came to him. The devil spoke to the Curé through this possessed person saying that he hated Saint John because he had robbed Satan of 120,000 souls. He claimed that if there were two more like the saintly priest, he would have to close up "business."

A young French atheist heard about the Curé of Ars, and out of curiosity, went to see him. The young man went back to his hometown full of faith, talking about God. A friend challenged him on his change of heart, and the young man replied that he now knew God exists because he saw God living in that priest. Saint John Vianney had a powerful ministry, but his many trials and sufferings were the price he paid for the conversion of souls.

Saint Padre Pio

Saint Padre Pio also had a powerful co-redemptive mission. He certainly had his sufferings, including his own encounters with Satan. One time he started doing an exorcism and halfway through told the person to come back the next day and he'd finish then. As Padre Pio walked away, the devil spoke through the possessed person saying that he hated Padre Pio and that he would get back at him that night. Sure enough, the friars he lived with heard a big commotion in Padre Pio's room that night and ran to see what the problem was. They found him on the floor, beaten head to foot but with a pillow under his head. He told his fellow friars that the devil had come and beaten him and thrown him down. Then, he said, the Blessed Mother had come, and when the devil threw him down she had put the pillow there so he wouldn't hurt his head!

Some of the friars were a little skeptical. However, the next day the possessed person returned. Before Padre Pio got there, the devil screamed through the person that he hated that priest and that he had gotten him the previous night. He claimed that he would have done more damage but the Woman in White, as he called Mary, came. The devil confirmed what Padre Pio said had happened. Interestingly, the devil will never pronounce the name of Mary because he and those who are with him hate her so much. To them, she is simply "the Woman in White."

Our Lady of Fatima's Plea

The world appears to be coming to some kind of great climax between the forces of good and evil. When Mary appeared to the children at Fatima, Portugal, in 1917, she promised that in the end, her Immaculate Heart would triumph. Her message is essentially a message of coredemptive love. She wanted to show that even the simplest people could understand her request, so she entrusted it to children.

Mary's message at Fatima centered on the coredemptive mission God has given to His Church. After Pope John Paul II was shot on the feast of Our Lady of Fatima, May 13, 1981, he read all the documentation on Fatima while he recuperated in the hospital. He concluded that the message of Fatima is more important now than it was in 1917.

What was Mary's message? The key to Fatima is the apparition that took place in July when the children saw the vision of hell. Afterward, Mary said to them: "You have seen hell where the souls of poor sinners go. To save them, God wishes to establish in the world devotion to my Immaculate Heart." In August, Mary told the children: "Pray, pray very much, and make sacrifices for sinners; for many souls go to hell, because there are none to sacrifice themselves and to pray for them."[1]

Prayer

Our Lady's requests at Fatima can be summarized as a call to prayer and sacrifice. Prayer for the conversion of sinners is absolutely essential, and the prayer Mary focused on was the rosary. In each visit, she spoke of the rosary as a powerful prayer that could bring about the conversion of sinners and the end to wars.

Are there people in your family in need of conversion? Have they drifted away from God? Pray the rosary daily and you will find that God's power will come and will grow stronger every day. Our Lady gave the children at Fatima a little prayer and asked that we say this at the end of each decade: "Oh my Jesus, forgive us our sins, save us from the fires of hell. Lead all souls to heaven, especially those who are most in need of your mercy." During the October apparition, just before the miracle in which the sun danced in the sky, Mary said, "I am the Lady of the Rosary. Continue always to pray the Rosary every day."[2] Prayer for the salvation of souls, especially the prayer of the rosary, is the first part of Our Lady's co-redemptive work.

Sacrifice

Our Lady also asked us to offer sacrifices for the conversion of sinners. The Angel of Peace, who had appeared to the children before Our Lady's apparitions began, also told them to offer sacrifices. Little Lucia asked the angel how they should do this, and the angel said: "Make of everything you can a sacrifice, and offer it to God as an act of reparation for the sins by which He is offended, and in supplication for the conversion of sinners."[3]

Saint Paul said: "Whatever you do, in word or deed, do everything in the name of the Lord Jesus" (Colossians 3:17). When we do even the ordinary activities of life out of love for Jesus, He will accept them and unite them to the deeds of His own life and death. In this way they take on co-redemptive power. Every morning we should offer to the Lord all our activities of the upcoming day—from eating a meal, to going to work, to cooking, to reading the newspaper. Anything we do, other than sin, can be offered as a sacrifice to the Lord. Saint Thérèse went so far as to offer God her heartbeats! She wanted every heartbeat to be an act of love for God because, as she said, she wanted to love Jesus as He had never been loved before.

God raised up Saint Thérèse to show us how to live the message of the gospel simply but intensely. She didn't work miracles or bilocate like Padre Pio. Like Mother Teresa, she had ordinary gifts but used them with great love, offering up everything as a sacrifice. As we, too, make sacrifices, we can add to these acts of love the sacrifice prayer Our Lady taught us at Fatima: "O Jesus, it is for love of You, for the conversion of sinners, and in reparation for the sins committed against the Immaculate Heart of Mary."[4]

As to the three visionaries of Fatima, they accepted all the trials that came their way and added their own sacrifices to them. They gracefully endured misunderstandings in their families and even the disapproval of the parish priest and the bishop who, anxious about the apparitions, told the children to stop lying. Their little acts of self-denial included giving away their homemade lunches and eating bitter chestnuts instead. The Blessed Mother appeared privately to Jacinta and said she would take her to heaven now or in six months if she chose to stay on earth a bit longer to save souls. Jacinta had been very disturbed by the vision of hell the children had seen; not wanting anyone to go there, she chose to stay and offered her sufferings for sinners.

Making sacrifices is also a way for us to avoid a self-absorbed holiness focused only on our own needs. We can pray and work not only for the conversion of family and friends but also for strangers. One of my professors in theology had been a missionary in Australia. He told the class that every year a woman came to the rectory and asked that Masses be offered for Joseph Stalin and Adolph Hitler. The reason, she said, was that so many people would simply write them off as eternally damned. But in the mercy of God, who knows—even they might be saved.

A very important sacrifice all of us can offer in our decadent culture is the sacrifice of chastity. Each of us is called to live chastely according to our vocation in life: whether we are married or single, whether we are consecrated celibates such as priests, sisters or brothers, or whether we are young or old, chastity is a virtue all are called to practice. The Curé of Ars said that, were it not for a few chaste souls, God would have destroyed the entire world long ago! The practice of this virtue involves a struggle to be chaste every day. We can offer this struggle as a sacrifice, faithfully living out God's call.

Years ago I saw a poster that said: "One person with a belief is equal in force to ninety-nine people who merely have an interest." When we believe in our faith, rather than merely having an interest in it, we become a witness and source of strength to others. You might be the only person in your office who refuses to curse and who won't participate in things that aren't right. You may be criticized. You may be shunned. But gradually some will begin to respect you and even in some cases admire you. People may even want to imitate you because you are willing to be a sign. At any rate, your sacrifices will count for much in the spiritual warfare in which we are engaged.

Christ said, "I have overcome the world" (John 16:33). Is the power of Satan stronger than the power of Christ? Not at all, so don't be afraid. Be faithful in prayer for others and offer sacrifices for them.

United With Christ

Often, when I think of the redemptive nature of suffering, I recall the story of Jesus feeding the crowd of five thousand with the five loaves and two fish that a boy in the crowd offered. Such a meager food supply seems unlikely to do much good. Yet Jesus in a real sense made Himself dependent upon this boy who gave so generously; Jesus multiplied that food and fed that immense group. That is what He also does with our prayers and sufferings. They seem very little in the face of the needs of the world, yet joined to His own sufferings, they take on that redemptive quality. Jesus uses them to redeem the world. This is redemptive suffering.

Jesus needs our suffering to use in redeeming souls. We need our suffering so that we can share with Him in the co-redemptive mission. The world needs it that none may be lost eternally from God's love.

• THE SUFFERING THAT PURIFIES US •

Aaccording to an old saying, suffering can make you better or bitter. It is, indeed, a double-edged sword. On the one hand, suffering can bring us closer to God, but on the other hand, it can move us further away from Him. It all depends on what we do with the suffering that comes our way.

Padre Pio used to say that everybody in life has a cross; the important thing, he said, is to use the cross like the good thief and not like the bad thief. The two thieves who were crucified with Jesus—Saint Dismas is the name traditionally given to the good thief—were so close to Jesus that they could talk with Him.

Gesmas, as the bad thief is sometimes called, said, "Are you not the Christ? Save yourself and us!" (Luke 23:39). This man was angry at his fate, but he wouldn't acknowledge his sins. Unfortunately, his bitter situation hardened his heart.

In contrast, grace was at work in Dismas. Initially, both thieves mocked Christ, but something happened that changed one. I think Dismas was transformed by the first words of Jesus from the cross: "Father, forgive them; for they know not what they do" (Luke 23:34).

We know from ancient sources that people crucified by the Romans cursed their executioners from the cross. Sometimes it became so bad that the Romans would cut out their tongues. And yet far from cursing, far from calling down evil, Jesus pleaded with the Father to forgive his tormentors.

In that moment, in the light offered by Christ as he was dying, I believe that Dismas saw his own sinfulness. In that light, he saw his own darkness. And this is what suffering can do. Embraced properly, it can enlighten and humble us.

To be humble is simply to know and accept the truth about ourselves. Dismas allowed his suffering to reveal the truth, to humble him, and when it did he encountered the mercy of Christ. He even rebuked the other thief for his mockery: "Do you not fear God, since you are under the same sentence of condemnation?...This man has done nothing wrong" (Luke 23:40–41).

Dismas, knowing himself to be a sinner, then turned to Jesus and said: "Jesus, remember me when you come into your kingdom" (Luke 23:42, NRSV). Dismas believed that Jesus, who seemed so helpless on that cross, could do something for him. And the Lord did, giving him the most beautiful promise in the Gospel: "Truly, I say to you, today you will be with me in Paradise" (Luke 23:43). Dismas allowed his suffering to lead him to the great mercy of God.

Embracing the Cross

The example of Dismas can help us avoid the anger, bitterness and self-pity that often accompany suffering, leading us to even worse sins such as violence, injustice, envy, infidelity and betrayal. When suffering comes, we must refuse to become embittered and we must root out any resentment we feel.

On the other hand, accepting suffering can make us better. People who have suffered well, maintaining a good attitude, are often more patient with the shortcomings of other people because they have been there, they know the struggle. Suffering can foster compassion, a word derived from two Latin words, *cum* (with) and *passio* (to endure, to experience, to go through). So, to have compassion means to experience or suffer with another person.

Nevertheless, embracing a cross is often difficult. Saint Teresa of Avila, however, says that once you embrace your cross, it's no longer a cross. This is because the most difficult thing about a cross is that we don't want it. But once we accept it and embrace it, it is no longer bitter and unwanted.

Saint Francis of Assisi, for example, put great emphasis on his encounter with a leper. Francis found lepers so repulsive that he couldn't bear to be near those who lived in the valley around Assisi. Whenever he met a leper on the road, he would ride away, holding his nose against the stench and averting his eyes from the nauseating sight.

Once his conversion was underway, though, he made Jesus a promise that he would do whatever the Lord asked. (Don't ever make that promise unless you mean it! You could pray for twenty-five years for someone's conversion and never see the slightest sign of progress, but if you tell the Lord that you will do anything He wants, I promise you, within twenty-four hours, you will be tested in your prayer.)

Francis was soon tested. He was out riding one day when, without warning, there on the road in front of him stood a leper. Francis wanted to do what he had always done and leave, but this time it was different. The Holy Spirit spoke to him in his heart and told him he must overcome himself. He must come to see that what he thought was bitter was really sweet.

Francis, in obedience, got off his horse, walked over to this leper who had his hand out for alms and, overcoming the aversion he must have felt, embraced the leper. He then put some coins in the leper's hands and, to show that he had fully accepted this poor and unfortunate man, he kissed his hand. When he got back on his horse and turned around, lo and behold, the leper was gone.

As Mother Teresa said so often, "Jesus comes to us in the distressing disguise of the poorest of the poor." And that's who Francis met on the road that day, Jesus in the distressing disguise of the poorest of the poor. Saint Francis said that after that his heart was filled with a sweetness that never left him. In fact, he went and worked among the lepers and even cured some of them miraculously. Later on, when other brothers joined his Order, Saint Francis assigned each brother to a leper so that they would learn, by taking care of that person, what he had learned by embracing the leper that day.

When we struggle with embracing our crosses, it's like Francis embracing that leper. It all seems so bitter, doesn't it? But once we embrace that cross, somehow the Holy Spirit can change our hearts and even bring a sweetness to the experience not because it is beautiful in itself, but because Jesus sent it to us. We are being purified when we embrace that cross because it makes us follow Christ more completely.

Getting Out of the Comfort Zone

Suffering well requires being patient with ourselves and others. That takes effort. We might not want to make that effort because we all have a certain tendency toward inertia. When an object is at rest, inertia is the force that keeps it at rest. If we are at rest and the Lord is asking us to get moving, that internal resistance, that spiritual inertia, holds us back.

Overcoming inertia is key, and we can start by confronting the everyday frustrations of life peaceably. Do you ever experience road rage? Somebody cuts you off on the road, someone speeds by, somebody tailgates, someone else leans on his horn and tries to force you over. It's easy to get enraged. You find yourself starting the litany, and it's not the litany of the saints!

Those negative feelings are our emotions rising up and expressing themselves. We're angry because someone has done something we feel is unjust or annoying. What do we do about that? The moment challenges us to overcome that anger if we are going to be Christlike. "Do not be overcome by evil," Saint Paul said, "but overcome evil with good" (Romans 12:21).

To choose a blessing rather than a curse, to choose to accept someone who causes me to suffer pain, to embrace an enemy or a spiritual leper, these are essential attitudes in the Christian life. We all have difficult people in our lives, either in our family or at work or where we shop or in our parish. Sometimes we deal with them primarily by avoiding them. They are people who challenge us, and so we stay in our own very comfortable zone, our circle of comfort. When somebody intrudes into that circle with his or her demands on our time, patience or whatever it may be, we suffer. Worse, we often react. That's when we have to overcome ourselves, like Saint Francis with the leper. When he listened to the Holy Spirit, he found sweetness in embracing the leper and found Jesus there in the distressing poor person before him.

When we go beyond ourselves, we achieve some measure of purification. Saint John tells us that "God is love" (1 John 4:16); when we break out of the self-love of our comfort zone and reach out to others, we imitate God and do what He is calling us to do. Love tends to give itself, and God is always giving Himself. If we are to become children of God, we have to go against the grain and reach out to others in compassion, patience and service. Doing so is not only purifying, it will also make our charity increase. As we have already seen, Saint Thérèse used to say, the food of real love is sacrifice!

Stages of Spiritual Growth

Understanding and accepting the role of suffering in the spiritual life takes time; even the apostles went through various stages on their way to accepting the teaching of Christ about the cross. Saint Augustine said that there are many Christians who can practice virtue and resist temptations; these are beginners who are learning how to overcome the temptations that had separated them from God. Then, he said, there are Christians who do good, practicing the corporal and spiritual works of mercy, for example. But, he says, many are not yet ready to suffer. That takes something more, a spiritual maturity that most often comes in stages.

Start at the Beginning

We see these stages unfold in the lives of the apostles. In the first stage they were like beginners in the life of faith. Every time the Lord mentioned the cross, they couldn't deal with it. Like most beginners encountering difficulties, they might have expressed some degree of patience, but basically they just wanted troubles or hints of troubles to go away as fast as possible.

The Gospels show us clearly that they often got impatient and even angry at people who annoyed them. For example, some of the apostles were probably among those who told the blind man, Bartimaeus, to keep quiet when he cried out to our Lord for help as Jesus was walking by (Mark 10:46–52). They complained to our Lord about the Caananite woman who was also crying out to our Lord in desperate need of His help (Matthew 15:21-28). They scolded the mothers and children who were coming to Jesus for His blessing, and even tried to stop them (Mark 10:13–16). James and John even wanted our Lord to call down fire and brimstone on a Samaritan village that would not welcome Him, for which our Lord nicknamed them "sons of thunder" (Luke 9:51–56; Mark 3:17).

The apostles ended up very holy, but at this point they still had a long way to go in their spiritual growth.

Acceptance and Resignation
The apostles entered the second stage of growth—acceptance of suffering—when Jesus was put to death on the cross and rose again. Then their attitude changed.

All their hope in Jesus had been set on an earthly kingdom in Israel; when our hearts are set on the things of this world, we can't come close to the true kingdom of God. Often, it's not until our hopes for this world are shattered that we are finally able to understand Jesus' mind and heart. But God has a way of helping people become free so that the world no longer attracts them. As He said, "No servant can serve two masters; for either he will hate the one and love the other, or he will be devoted to the one and despise the other. You cannot serve God and mammon" (Luke 16:13).

As we let go of the world, we can embrace Jesus and see what He is calling us to. Jesus then starts to attract us. This is what happened to the apostles when Jesus died on the cross and their hopes for an earthly kingdom were shattered.

This second stage in the spiritual life is marked by an acceptance of or resignation to suffering. Christians in this stage of growth are more able to let go of resentful or bitter feelings, to quit rehearsing in their minds and hearts all the negative things they've experienced that keep the hurt alive.

A friar once told me that he was a troubleshooter in his province. He went to various houses of his province to see how things were going and to assess possible problems. At one friary an old priest came to talk to him. This old friar complained that the superior was terrible, that the friars didn't treat him with respect and so on. The friar who was listening knew that this superior would never treat this old friar poorly, and he knew that the friars he lived with were not unkind. So he asked him, "Father, when did these things happen?" The old friar responded, "Fifty years ago." But he talked about it as if it had happened five days ago.

You can destroy those old tapes that play in your mind by accepting your situation and making your peace. Resignation means that you accept the fact that there were difficulties in your life and things didn't go the way you wanted. But you choose not to live the rest of your life with negative feelings. You've got to move on. That is what it means to make your peace with your past and your present. Resigned to what the Lord has sent and maybe is still sending you, you embrace the disappointments and hurts and deal with them as best you can.

Abandonment to God

After Jesus ascended into heaven, the apostles reached the third stage of growth, abandonment to God. They went to Jerusalem, according to His instructions: "Behold, I send the promise of my Father upon you, but stay in the city, until you are clothed with power from on high" (Luke 24:49). They were not ready to go forth to do His work until they received God's promise, the gift of the Holy Spirit.

They went back to the upper room with the Blessed Mother and "devoted themselves to prayer" (Acts 1:14). They prayed for nine days—the first novena—and at the end, "suddenly a sound came from heaven like the rush of a mighty wind...and they were all filled with the Holy

Spirit" (Acts 2:2, 4). In an instant, their lives were changed and in that moment they received a new gift, the ability to give themselves and their futures over to God. In the spiritual life, we call this *abandonment*–giving the Lord control of our life.

Joy in Suffering

With the descent of the Holy Spirit, the apostles finally received the ability to find joy in suffering. The Holy Spirit changed them so radically that these followers of Jesus, who had once been afraid to suffer, would now suffer with joy for the sake of the Lord. They had come a long way, enduring the great sadness of Jesus' death on their way to the Resurrection. Archbishop Sheen used to say that there is no Easter Sunday without a Good Friday, and we, too, can be confident that when we suffer for Christ, we will rise with Him in joy.

We see the apostles' change of heart when they were brought before the Sanhedrin. Scripture tells us that this council was "enraged and wanted to kill them" (Acts 5:33) but a Pharisee named Gamaliel intervened. He said that if the apostles' work was merely human, it would fail, "but if it is of God, you will not be able to overthrow them. You might even be found opposing God!" (Acts 5:39). The council took his advice and let the apostles go, but had them beaten first. The apostles left the presence of the Sanhedrin rejoicing that they had been found worthy to suffer for Christ. Strengthened by the Spirit, they experienced joy in suffering.

Why? Not because they found pleasure in pain. That is sadism and must be avoided; it has nothing to do with Christian joy. The apostles' joy sprang from deep love. What was true for them is true for us: When we love deeply, suffering is no longer a burden.

I learned about love from the great example of my own mother. Once when I was about eleven years old, I became extremely sick and nearly got pneumonia. I was so sick I couldn't get to my room, and instead I stayed on a couch in our living room. My mother stayed up the whole night with me just to make sure that I would be all right. Was it painful for her? Certainly! Did she complain about it? Absolutely not, because she didn't measure the experience in terms of her pain. She measured it in terms of her love for her son!

Love doesn't ask, "How difficult is it? How much do I have to give?" Love doesn't count the cost. As Saint Paul said, "Love bears all things, believes all things, hopes all things, endures all things" (1 Corinthians 13:7). It gives of itself because God gives of Himself, and when we imitate Him in this, regardless of the circumstances, we will find joy.

Athletes often say, "No pain; no gain." In other words, if you don't push yourself beyond your current level of endurance, you will not progress. Comparing himself to an athlete, Saint Paul wrote that he forgets what lies behind: "Straining forward to what lies ahead, I press on toward the goal for the prize of the upward call of God in Christ Jesus" (Philippians 3:14). So we, as followers of Christ, press forward in our daily struggles, enduring through the cross with Jesus. This is what makes us saints.

• WHAT MIGHT MY CROSS LOOK LIKE? •

Life in this world is a test, a trial, and everyone has a cross of some kind to bear. As Scripture says, "...when you come to serve the LORD, / prepare yourself for trials" (Sirach 2:1, NAB). The trial of life consists in this: will we love God and His ways or ourselves and our own ways? Archbishop Sheen would say that there are basically two philosophies of life, the Christian and the secular. In the Christian, first you fast, and then you feast. We have our trials now, but we look for eternal joy in heaven. According to the secular philosophy, first you feast, and then comes the hangover!

Our sufferings test us, but they are all tailor-made to bring us closer to God. When God sends a cross, it applies uniquely to our own situation. There is a reflection, often attributed to Saint Francis de Sales, that expresses this truth eloquently.

The everlasting God has in His wisdom foreseen from eternity the cross that He now presents to you as gift from His inmost heart. This cross He now sends you He has considered with His all-knowing eyes, understood with His divine mind, tested with His wise justice, warmed with loving arms and weighed with His own hands to see that it be not one inch too large and not one ounce too heavy for you. He has blessed it with His holy name, anointed it with His consolation, taken one last glance at you and your courage, and then sent it to you from heaven, a special greeting from God to you, an alms of the all-merciful love of God.[1]

Be content with the cross that you have received, and try to do your best to carry it with Jesus. Don't worry if your cross looks different from someone else's or if another person's cross seems smaller. There is a story about a man who complained that his cross was too big. He complained so much that God finally said, "All right, go into that warehouse over there and pick any cross you want." He went into the warehouse where he saw some huge crosses. He figured his must have been one of those. He looked around, found a tiny cross and said to God, "I'll take that one." God said, "That's the one you just had!" Keep in mind that God gives us the cross we can bear and that many people carry much bigger crosses than we do. Don't wish for someone else's set of circumstances because you never know what a person is enduring.

Even something that appears to be good fortune can turn out to be a cross. I know of a couple who won the lottery and after taxes received about half a million dollars. With all that money came heartache: Their kids got into drugs, two of them ended up in jail and problems came into the marriage. The mother told one of my relatives that the worst day in her family's life was the day they won the lottery.

So you never know. There is an old saying: "God orders all things sweetly." He will give us the grace to handle our crosses well.

Personal Crosses

What might a cross look like? Maybe it consists of physical sickness or injury. These are crosses, even if they only temporarily disrupt our lives. Chronic illness is definitely a demanding cross. And of course the deprivations of old age are crosses—the gradual loss of hearing, sight, strength and, for some, the onset of dementia.

Sometimes our personal crosses are more of an emotional nature, and we find ourselves fighting fears and anxieties, depression and loneliness. God, in giving us these very difficult crosses, is asking us to learn to trust Him and His never-failing care for us. Some people are beset by the problem of perfectionism. The temptation to have to be perfect in everything we do is a real trial that might take years and years to overcome.

Spiritual problems can also be a cross. People who love God very deeply might enter a period of dryness in prayer. Unable to feel God's presence, they think that He has abandoned them or doesn't love them. I'm reminded of the beautiful Song of Solomon in the Old Testament that describes the love between a bride and groom. At one point, the bride, searching for the bridegroom but unable to find him, says, "Have you seen him whom my soul loves?" (Song of Solomon 3:3). Sometimes we, too, experience that sense of loss and we wonder: Where is He whom we love? Doesn't He love me anymore?

This is a very powerful trial but we must remember that God never walks away from us. He may be silent, we might not sense His presence, but He is near and His love never wavers. God doesn't have moods; He doesn't wear a mood ring to find out if He is going to have a good day or a bad day. He loves you as much on the worst day of your life as He loves you on the best. God doesn't have moods; we do!

As we saw earlier, Mother Teresa endured fifty years of spiritual dryness and experienced this sense of abandonment by God. Saint Thérèse of Lisieux similarly entered a dark night of suffering for about eighteen months before her death and said that she experienced no consolation from God. Both these women—and countless other Christians—have endured this sense of abandonment but have weathered the storm by carrying their cross and seeking the Lord with all their heart.

Old habits of sin can come back and haunt people; these severe crosses test us but can be borne just like any other cross. In these situations, it often helps to seek the counsel of a wise confessor and the grace of the sacraments as an aid in getting through the temptations. Sometimes when people get older, the devil brings up their past sins and says that God didn't forgive them. The dark night and sense of desolation that can accompany these trials are part of the cross. God leads us through these trials so that we learn to trust Him more, to love Him more and to seek Him with holy longing.

Sometimes our family is the source of our cross. Those who are married must keep in mind that their commitment is for better or worse, for richer or poorer, in sickness and in health, until death. Separation and even civil divorce happen at times when, for example, a spouse or children need protection from abuse. But the struggles of married life are crosses allowed by God to help a couple grow together in holiness. We learn to love God through loving one another; this begins in the family.

I like to tell the story of a priest who was giving a parish mission. He told the people to bring any religious articles they wanted blessed on the last night of the mission and he would bless them. The night came, and he asked everyone to hold up all their religious articles. A big commotion broke out in the back of the church because a woman was trying to lift up her husband. The priest said, "Lady, I'm not blessing people; I'm blessing religious articles." She yelled back, "Father, he's my cross!"

Raising children, too, can be a cross. Criticism, fighting, the loss of respect and the use of foul language can crowd into a family's life and do great harm. Parents and children need to work and pray together to achieve harmony. Sometimes, no matter how faithfully and lovingly parents carry out their role, disappointments, troubles, alienation from the family, ingratitude, abandonment of the faith and other problems can occur when the children grow up.

Numerous daily irritations can accumulate to feel like quite a heavy cross. Conflicts at work, different approaches to problems and lack of communication can be terrible burdens that weigh us down and rob us of joy. I remember a cartoon that fits in here. A man was reading the newspaper while his wife was working on a crossword puzzle. He is saying to her, in answer to her question: "No, I don't know the meaning of the word *apathy* and I couldn't care less." That kind of attitude, especially in families, can be very painful.

Finally, the world presents us with crosses in the form of war, terrorism, the economy, natural disasters and so on.

The Crosses of Padre Pio

Some people are chosen by God to be victim souls, asked to bear great suffering for the love of Christ. This type of suffering is called "witness suffering." These men and women give a good example of faithful Christian life that encourages us.

Padre Pio was such a person. He had many sufferings, but he used to ask the Lord for more because he wanted to share in those of Christ. He endured the cross of illness, beginning with a bronchial condition that started in childhood and remained with him for life. He sometimes had fevers of 115 degrees! He served in the military during World War I but was sent home to recuperate on five occasions, the last time, according to the doctor, so that he could die in peace!

Misunderstanding and false accusations plagued him, even in childhood. When he was a young boy, someone slipped a love note into his pocket during class in order to play a trick on him. The other kids, amused, made a lot of noise, and when the teacher asked them what was going on, they said, "It's Francesco [his baptismal name], he's in love!" The teacher found the love note and slapped him. Later the teacher learned what had really happened and apologized to Francesco. Years later, Padre Pio, referring to that incident, noted that the teacher never took the slap back!

When Francesco was getting ready to go to the seminary, a student who was jealous of him started a rumor that Francesco was in love with the train master's daughter. The parish priest, who was helping Francesco with his preparations, never asked him directly about it. The priest became so angry, though, that he kept his distance and wouldn't communicate with Francesco for an entire month. The poor young man didn't know what was going on. Later, the priest learned the truth and helped Francesco along with his plans.

Later in life, the Holy Office placed Padre Pio under investigation five times in a period of ten years, all because people, including his local archbishop, spoke against him. He bore the stigmata—the five wounds of Christ—in his hands, feet and side for fifty years. Some people, though, accused him of faking these wounds. One, a priest who was also a psychiatrist, wanted to investigate these wounds even though the Holy See had forbidden anyone to investigate them without explicit permission from the Vatican. Padre Pio asked the priest if he had this permission, but the priest would only say that the Holy Office knew he was there. Padre Pio pointed out that he hadn't asked that; he had asked if he had permission. When the priest said, "no," Padre Pio threw him out.

Unfortunately, the priest went back to Rome and told Pope Pius XI that they were hiding a fake in that monastery. Subsequently placed under investigation, Padre Pio couldn't speak with his usual spiritual director. In fact, he didn't speak to him again until that man was on his deathbed and Padre Pio, using bilocation, appeared at his bedside.

He was also forbidden to have any contact with his spiritual children. But worst of all his trials were the two years he was forbidden to say Mass publicly and to hear confessions. He used to weep and wonder what he had done to deserve such punishments.

These trials ended when a new archbishop for the

region went to Rome and asked the pope why he was treating Padre Pio so severely. The pope said that he had been told he was a fake. This archbishop corrected that impression. Later, even the psychiatrist who had accused him of faking his wounds asked Padre Pio's forgiveness. The Padre did forgive him, but warned the priest that he had better pray that God forgive him!

The stigmata itself was physically painful. Someone once asked Padre Pio if his wounds hurt, and he said, sure they do. God didn't give them to him for good looks! I knew a man who was present when a pilgrim reached out and grabbed Padre Pio's hand. Padre Pio screamed in pain because of the open wound.

Finally, along with all these sufferings, Padre Pio also endured beatings from the devil. I remember seeing a photograph taken two weeks after one of these incidents; the beating had been so severe that Padre Pio still had two black eyes.

Saint Padre Pio was a true disciple of Jesus. He daily took up his cross in its many forms, and faithfully followed after Jesus (Luke 9:23).

The Cross Carries Us

A passage in *The Imitation of Christ* notes that if we carry the cross, the cross will end up carrying us. In other words, the cross will strengthen us and make us less susceptible to the snares of the world.

It takes time and effort to learn to carry the cross with Jesus. Like the apostles, we learn to do this over time; in doing so, we learn to know and love Jesus, to enter not only into His sufferings but also into His joy.

We might wonder, after all this, if it is wrong to ask the Lord to take away our crosses. Jesus Himself gave the answer to that question in the Garden of Gethsemane: "Father, if you are willing, remove this cup from me; yet, not my will but yours be done" (Luke 22:42, NRSV). So yes, we may ask God to remove our crosses so long as we ask it according to his will.

Saint Teresa of Avila, when she was very young, had a great cross of sickness, and she prayed to the Lord to take it away. Later on she said that she thought she had made a mistake; she should have learned to carry that cross as best she could. While it lasted, God taught her many things through that cross and gave her many blessings.

Ask the Lord and Our Blessed Lady to give you strength to bear your crosses. They will bring you many graces, and they will bring your loved ones many graces as well. It is through bearing our crosses that God pours forth His grace more abundantly upon the world.

• THE VALUE OF SUFFERING IN OUR LIVES •

Mother Teresa of Calcutta used to say that when suffering comes, it is a sign that we are close enough to the cross of Jesus for Him to give us a kiss. One day, as she talked to a woman who had many crosses, she pointed out that these were a sign of Jesus' love for her. The woman turned to her and said, "Mother, please tell Jesus not to love me so much."

The cross is a tough but essential message; the cross itself is the very symbol of our faith, revered through the centuries. The Roman emperor Constantine was a pagan when, in the year 312, he faced a battle over control of the western empire. The night before this battle at the Milvian Bridge, Constantine had a vision in which he saw a cross in the sky, emblazoned in light. Around the cross were the words, "In this sign you shall conquer." He ordered the sign of the cross put on the armor of all the soldiers in his army, and they marched into battle and won.

The cross is the sign of Christ's victory. A priest, when he conducts an exorcism, uses a cross because this is such a powerful means of confronting Satan; the demons are afraid of the cross of Christ. Jesus transformed this symbol of suffering, humiliation and death into a symbol of hope, life and promise.

Jesus Predicts His Cross

Jesus preached about the cross three times during His public ministry, predicting that He would suffer and die on the cross but that He would rise again. The first occasion came after Jesus asked His disciples who people thought He was. They said some people thought He was John the Baptist, some Elijah, others Jeremiah and still others, one of the prophets.

Then He asked, "'But who do you say that I am?' Simon Peter answered, 'You are the Messiah, the Son of the living God.' And Jesus answered him, 'Blessed are you, Simon son of Jonah! For flesh and blood has not revealed this to you, but my Father in heaven. And I tell you, you are Peter, and on this rock I will build my church'" (Matthew 16:15–18, NRSV).

Now that the disciples knew that Jesus was the Messiah, He had to tell them what kind of Messiah He was going to be—a suffering Messiah, betrayed by His own people. At this revelation, Peter pulls Jesus aside and begins to remonstrate with Him "God forbid it, Lord! This must never happen to you" (Matthew 16:22, NRSV). He's trying to talk Him out of the cross! Jesus replies, "Get behind me, Satan! You are a stumbling block to me; for you are setting your mind not on divine things but on human things" (16:23, NRSV).

On the second occasion, the apostles were afraid to question Jesus about the predictions He made about His suffering (Mark 9:32). They were soon lost in arguing among themselves about which one of them was the greatest.

On the third occasion, Jesus explicitly told the apostles that they were headed for Jerusalem where "the Son of man will be delivered to the chief priests and scribes, and they will condemn him to death, and deliver him to the Gentiles to be mocked and scourged and crucified, and he will be raised on the third day" (Matthew 20:18-19). The Gospel of Luke tells us that "they [the apostles] understood none of these things...they did not grasp what was said" (Luke 18:34).

Clearly the apostles hoped that Jesus would be an earthly messiah who would drive out the Romans and reestablish the kingdom of Israel as it had been under King David and King Solomon. Those were the glory years and they yearned for them. But that wasn't Jesus' plan. For Him, the cross was everything.

Fire on the Earth

Jesus said, "I came to cast fire upon the earth; and would that it were already kindled!" (Luke 12:49). He was referring to the Holy Spirit, the fire of love who would dispel the coldness of the world and transform hearts that are selfish into loving hearts. He continued: "I have a baptism to be baptized with; and how I am constrained until it is accomplished!" (Luke 12:50). Not the baptism of John, since that had already taken place; rather Jesus was talking about the baptism of His death. It was only through the death and resurrection of Jesus that we were "sealed with the promised Holy Spirit, who is the guarantee of our inheritance" (Ephesians 1:13–14).

In a sense, when a person dies we could say he is victimized by death; death wraps its chains around him. Jesus destroyed those chains by dying and then rising from the dead and entering into His glory at the Father's right hand. In turn, the Father glorified Jesus by sending us the Spirit.

When people die at a relatively old age, we feel that they have lived out their life and have accomplished what they had to accomplish. But if someone dies relatively young, especially if death comes suddenly, we feel regret that the person didn't have a full life. In the natural course of events, it would seem that death came too soon for Jesus, who was only thirty-three. After all, look at all the good He was doing—healing the sick, raising the dead, freeing people from evil spirits, preaching the gospel.

And yet, His death was the very goal of His life. The Lord freely laid down His life and endured suffering to fulfill His Father's will. His death did not curtail His message; it fulfilled it. Jesus was not a helpless victim in the face of His enemies. He could have wiped Pilate and the whole Roman army off the face of the earth so completely that no one would have even remembered they existed. He could have summoned twelve legions of angels to defeat His enemies. But it was the Father's will to redeem the world by allowing His own Son to endure the cross. As Archbishop Sheen said, Jesus Christ was the only man ever born into the world in order to die.

Saint Paul and the Cross

Saint Paul preached in Athens, a city known for its love of new ideas. He gave the citizens there a fancy sermon, quoting some of their philosophers and speaking in a manner that he thought would please these people. They were attentive until he mentioned the resurrection of the body.

Greek philosophy tended to look down on the body. Plato, one of the great Greek philosophers, said that our souls existed before our bodies. When the souls sinned, God punished them by imprisoning them in bodies. The Greeks couldn't wait for the soul to be set free from the body. And here was Paul saying that in the end, Jesus will raise our body and reunite it with our soul. To the Greek mind, this was jarring; many of them scoffed (Acts 17:18–34).

Saint Paul went next to the cosmopolitan city of Corinth. Corinth was something of a "sin city," a seaport, with a temple to the goddess Aphrodite that housed many temple prostitutes. Paul might have been uneasy, especially following his experience in Athens, but in fact he had great success. Jesus said to him in a vision: "Do not be afraid, but speak and do not be silent; for I am with you, and no man shall attack you to harm you" (Acts 18:9-10).

In Corinth, Paul took a different approach in his preaching: "When I came to you, brethren, I did not come proclaiming to you the testimony of God in lofty words or wisdom. For I decided to know nothing among you except Jesus Christ and him crucified" (1 Corinthians 2:1-2).

It came down to this for Paul: "Jews demand signs and Greeks seek wisdom, but we preach Christ crucified, a stumbling block to Jews and folly to Gentiles, but to those who are called, both Jews and Greeks, Christ the power of God and the wisdom of God" (1 Corinthians 1:22-24). To the Jews, the crucifixion of Jesus was a scandal. They could not believe that their own religious leaders would reject the Messiah whom they awaited. The Greeks, with their pantheon of all-powerful gods, felt it was absolutely absurd to think of God being at the mercy of human beings.

These objections are still with us. I once stopped for gas on the New York Thruway and a Sikh, seeing my habit, asked what I was. I said, "I'm a Catholic priest," and he said, "Oh, all religions are good: Jewish religion good, Christian religion good, Muslim religion *very* good." He added: "Abraham prophet, Jesus prophet, Mohammed *great* prophet." I said, "We don't believe that; we believe that Jesus Christ is the Son of God." He said, "Crazy idea!"

Notice that what was crazy to this fellow was the idea that God became man. So many people equate God with power and can't get their minds around the idea of a God who would become weak. Mercy and humility are seen as weaknesses. So the notion of a suffering, crucified God who became one of us is considered crazy.

The Cross: A Powerful Teaching Instrument

The cross will teach us great things. Don't be afraid to stand in spirit at the foot of that cross with Our Blessed Lady, with Saint John and Saint Mary Magdalene. You will be amazed at what you will learn if you open your heart and ask God to help you understand why God loved you so much that He died for you. It is only at the foot of the cross that we begin to understand that suffering, as Mother Teresa said, is a kiss from the cross of Jesus.

The cross is a tough topic because that is where we learn about tough love. Jesus didn't love suffering for its own sake and neither should we. Suffering for its own sake has no meaning whatsoever. But the suffering sanctified by Jesus Christ—and our suffering in union with Him—has great power and great wisdom.

Saint Bonaventure, the Franciscan Doctor of the Church, called the cross the new staff of Moses. When Moses came to the Red Sea, God told him to lift up his staff and part the waters of the sea with it (Exodus 14:16). He did so and the Israelites escaped the Egyptians over the dry ground. Saint Bonaventure said that the cross of

Jesus is the new staff. With that staff Jesus has parted not the sea, allowing people to journey to the Promised Land; rather he has opened the doors to the kingdom of heaven that were closed by the sin of our first parents. With that new staff, the cross, He has opened the way to eternal life.

• THE HEART OF MARY •

My parents were married on September 15, the feast of Our Lady of Sorrows. When I was a child, I thought it was an unusual day to choose for a wedding, but my parents were devout Catholics. The parish where my father grew up even had a sodality of women called Our Lady of Sorrows Sodality. My parents realized—and gradually I did too—that Mary is our Mother, both in our joys and in our sorrows.

Devotion to the Immaculate Heart of Mary was a central focus at Fatima where the children saw Mary's heart encircled by thorns that pierced it. On October 13, 1917, they also saw an apparition of Our Lady of Sorrows. Mary's Immaculate Heart and her Sorrowful Heart go together. Much of the reparation for sin called for at Fatima was for offenses against the Immaculate Heart of Mary. In 1925 Mary appeared to Lucia, with the child Jesus. Again, Mary's heart was surrounded by thorns. Jesus asked that people do penance and pray that these thorns be removed. To accomplish this, Our Lady asked for the establishment of the First Saturday devotion. This consisted of confession, Communion, the rosary and fifteen minutes of meditation on the mysteries of the rosary on five consecutive first Saturdays, with the intention of making reparation for the offenses against Mary's Immaculate Heart.

The Plan of Redemption

Mary, of course, could not redeem us, but she was certainly an accomplice to the Redemption. We can see this fact in part when we consider how the Fathers of the Church described the pattern of redemption.

The Fathers compared the Fall with the Redemption, pointing out that God redeemed the world according to a pattern that mirrored the devil's pattern in bringing about the Fall. God wanted to beat the devil at his own game, so to speak. There were three elements in the Fall: Adam, Eve and the Tree of the Knowledge of Good and Evil.

Adam represented the human race; he was the father of humanity. In the Redemption, Jesus, the new Adam, represents us. Eve was an accomplice to the Fall, eating the fruit and giving it to her husband. Although Mary could not redeem us, she was an accomplice to the Redemption, leading Jesus toward the cross. We see this clearly when Mary asked Jesus to help the young couple at the wedding feast at Cana. She told Him they had run out of wine. He said that this wasn't a concern of His because His "hour [had] not yet come" (John 2:4). He put His mother to a great test there. In the Gospel of John, the "hour" is always the hour of darkness for Satan, but it is the hour of victory for Christ, the hour of His cross.

Just as Eve of old gave the fruit to Adam, Mary led Jesus to the cross. When Mary's faith moved Jesus to work that miracle, she started Him on the way toward His "hour," which was the time of His suffering and death. As Archbishop Sheen pointed out in one of his talks, here we have a mother sending her own son onto a battlefield.

The Tree of the Knowledge of Good and Evil in the Old Testament becomes the Tree of the Cross in the New Testament. The tree from which Adam and Eve ate was a symbol of evil, suffering and degradation. The Tree of the Cross on which Jesus hung became the means of redemption. So God reversed the Fall, giving us Jesus for Adam, Mary for Eve and the cross for the forbidden tree.

Saint John Chrysostom said, in this regard:

You have observed his outstanding triumph, the splendid achievement of the cross. Now let me tell you something even more remarkable, the manner in which he gained his victory, and you will marvel all the more. Christ conquered the devil using the same means and same weapons that the devil used to win.

Let me tell you how this occurred. The symbols of our fall were a virgin, a tree and death. The virgin was Eve (for she had not yet known man); then there was the tree; and death was Adam's penalty. And again these three tokens of our destruction, the virgin, the tree and death, became the tokens of our victory. Instead of Eve there was Mary; instead of the tree of the knowledge of good and evil, the wood of the cross; instead of Adam's death, the death of

Christ. Do you see then that the devil was defeated by the very means he used to conquer? By a tree the devil laid Adam low, and by a tree Christ defeated him.[1]

Since our Blessed Lady plays a key role in the Redemption as the new Eve, she had to share with Jesus the suffering of the cross. She had no original sin, the source of suffering in the world, and so was spared the guilt of that sin. She was not, however, spared the sufferings resulting from that sin!

The Seven Sorrows of Mary

Catholics traditionally focus their devotion on Mary's Seven Sorrows in reverence for her spiritual martyrdom.

The first sorrow occurred when Mary and Joseph brought Jesus into the temple and the old man, Simeon, moved by the Holy Spirit, took the child into his arms and thanked God, saying, "Now, Master, you may let your servant go in peace, according to your word, for my eyes have seen your salvation" (Luke 2:29–30, NAB). Simeon then told Mary and Joseph that the child was destined to be a light to the nations and the glory of Israel, and they marveled at this. Then he said to Mary, "[T]his child is destined for the fall and rise of many in Israel, and to be a sign that will be contradicted (and you yourself a sword will pierce)" (Luke 2:34–35, NAB). Simeon was predicting the rejection of Jesus by many and the immense suffering this would bring to Our Lady.

The second sorrow occurred when King Herod tried to destroy the child Jesus and the Holy Family had to flee into Egypt. Mary's Son was now the object of hatred and of rejection by the world.

The child Jesus lost in the temple constitutes the third sorrow. Sometimes we share Mary's sorrow in this loss when we feel that the Lord is not with us. But like Our Lady, we must seek Him in our sorrow and not cease until we find Him during this "dark night of the soul."

The fourth sorrow of Mary commemorates the time she met Jesus as He carried His cross. The movie *The Passion of the Christ* brings this moment powerfully to light: When Jesus falls and His mother goes to help Him, there is a beautiful flashback of the child Jesus falling and Mary going to lift Him up.

The fifth sorrow focuses on Mary standing at the foot of the cross, seeing her own Son die. She willingly offered up her Son and stayed with Him to the end.

In the sixth sorrow, Mary receives the body of Jesus in her arms. Michaelangelo's Piéta movingly depicts this harrowing moment, as the sorrowing mother holds her dead Son.

The seventh sorrow commemorates Mary witnessing the burial of Jesus in the tomb. Mary alone held to belief in the Resurrection, even as they closed up Jesus' tomb. That's why she doesn't go with Mary Magdalene and the other women or run with John and Peter to the tomb on

Easter morning. She believed. She alone of all Jesus' disciples kept alive the belief of Jesus' resurrection from Good Friday to Easter Sunday.

The Sorrows of Mary give us hope; we know where to turn when we are in trouble. We go to our Mother because we know that she will be there for us. This is what Our Lady of Guadalupe said to Saint Juan Diego in 1531 when she requested a church be built on the site of her apparitions: "I can be present and give my love, compassion, help, and defense, for I am your most devoted mother...to hear your laments and to remedy all your miseries, pains, and sufferings."[2]

In the Eastern Churches they say that when Saint Andrew died and went to heaven, his brother Peter was already on the job. Andrew said to Peter, "Where is she?" Peter understood that he was asking for Our Lady. He replied, "Andrew, she's not up here in heaven. She's down on earth, drying the tears from the eyes of her children in the valley of tears."

So go to your Mother. She is with you, helping and comforting you as you share in the cross of Jesus. She is our Mother present in our sorrows. But as Jesus said, He will come, and "your sorrow will turn into joy" (John 16:20). Let us trust Mary and seek her intercession because she can help us love and understand the wisdom and the power of the cross of her Son. She had faithfully and lovingly stood below it!

• Joy: An Important Safeguard for Our Spiritual Lives •

The existential philosopher Friedrich Nietzsche would not be described as a friend of Christians. His famous phrase, "God is dead," summed up his opposition to all things religious. It was to become a rallying cry for the removal of God from all public life, a fact that is evident today in the secularizing trends of Western culture. Likewise, his glorification of the "superman" and the "Superrace" contributed significantly to the terrible tragedy of Nazism.

In addition to all this, Nietzsche put forth some direct challenges to Christian believers. One of them is a remark aimed primarily at our ability to attract nonbelievers to the faith: "Better songs would they have to sing, for me to believe in their Saviour: more like saved ones would his disciples have to appear unto me!"[1]

Have you ever been so happy that you burst out singing? Singing gives expression to a hidden joy in the soul. Joy, in turn, is characteristic of those who have found something significant that not only satisfies and fulfills them but also overflows outward to others.

Nietzsche's point is that the lives and attitudes of those who say they believe in Jesus and who claim to follow Him do not look very happy; they are not singing better songs! This is the reason our witness does not bear fruit. Joy saves the heart from feelings of emptiness, restlessness, sadness or depression.

This is all the more significant when we realize that all Christians are called to convince others that knowing and loving Jesus will bring them fulfillment and great joy. What a disappointment and even contradiction for the Christian to lack joy.

It seems fitting, then, to close a book about the challenges of prayer, charity and suffering involved in following Christ with a look at the joy that should permeate the life of every Christian. If this essential ingredient is missing in our lives, we will fall short of all that God has for us.

The joy of Christian faith starts from within. Saint Francis knew the importance of joy as a powerful weapon in spiritual warfare and said that the devil can't harm the servant of God whom he sees filled with holy joy. The saint taught that the devil goes around scattering the dust of sadness and discouragement—that "Babylonian stuff" he called it in reference to the sorrow of the Jewish people during their exile in Babylon. They couldn't even sing the songs of the Lord in this foreign land (Psalm 137:4). If we are covered with the armor of joy, however, the devil scatters his Babylonian dust in vain.

Spiritual Sadness

On the other hand, if we lack the armor of joy, we can easily become victimized by a sadness that also repels others. Saint Francis said that the devil rejoices most when he can steal the joy out of the heart of the servant of God. The saint understood that one sad Christian can easily infect others with sadness. Whenever he would see a sad friar, he would tell him that he had no right to inflict his sadness on all the others, bringing their spirits down. Often he would tell such a sad friar to go away and pray until he got his joy back. Then he could safely come and join the other brethren.

Spiritual sadness was one of the eight "thoughts" or demons that the desert fathers said could tempt them and us, too. This list included pride, vanity, avarice, gluttony, lust, anger, *acedia* (listlessness or apathy) and spiritual sadness. Saint Gregory the Great later rearranged this list into what we call the seven capital sins. He first reduced it by dropping vanity, which was close to pride. He next restricted *acedia* to sloth or laziness. He reduced spiritual sadness to envy, which is a sadness at the good of another.

The desert monks, however, had taught that spiritual sadness is much broader than the sadness of envy. It is a general sadness which brings an unhappiness that seems to paralyze the soul and weigh it down in sorrow. Such sadness can easily be an obstacle to one's personal spiritual growth as well as to one's witness to Christ.

What, then, are some forms of spiritual sadness that we are likely to encounter? First, there is the sadness of discouragement, which produces a readiness to give up when we encounter difficulties. We all have to deal with potential discouragement. Often it comes from a lack of apparent results when, for example, no matter how much we pray and sacrifice for a situation, nothing seems to change. The time lapse between the sowing of the seed of God's Word and the reaping of its harvest can often seem like an eternity. Don't watch the clock! Be persistent in your prayer or other efforts, but also keep busy in new fields of endeavor. Jesus assures us that the seed of God's word sprouts and grows without the farmer being aware of it (Mark 4:27). Developing an ability to smile while we wait certainly helps!

Sometimes sadness springs from a sense of weariness and boredom, especially when we are called to give an effort over and above the ordinary. Seeing the price tag for real Christianity, some go into an emotional slump! Saint Paul, on the other hand, says that God loves a "cheerful giver" (2 Corinthians 9:7). We can lighten the burden by realistically accepting the efforts and sacrifices demanded. The last thing we want to do is to fall into an attitude of self-pity, rehearsing over and over again in our minds all the efforts we have to put out. That is guaranteed to make life so much more difficult than it really is.

Still another potential source of sadness comes from a

negative spirit that leads us to complain when everything is not "just right." We must not naïvely expect that everything will work out smoothly all the time. In our Christian walk, for example, we are bound to meet people whose personalities have very sharp edges. We must be careful not to let them get under our skin. Even more, we must avoid an argumentative attitude.

Spiritual joy eases our burdens, protects from discouragement and gives a lightheartedness to everyday life. It also can keep us "singing." This is brought out in one of my favorite stories in the life of Saint Francis.

In the early days of his conversion, Francis went about one day, like a troubadour of the Lord, singing His praises in French in the Assisi countryside. Suddenly a group of thieves came upon him. When they asked him who he was, Saint Francis, barefoot and dressed in a poor penitent's tunic, answered that he was a herald of the great King.

We can only imagine how stunned the thieves were by his appearance and his answer! Then, mockingly, they began to laugh at him. One of the thieves pushed him into a ditch filled with melting snow and mud and said, "Lay there, you herald of the great King!" They went off, laughing at one they considered a religious fool. What did Saint Francis do? He picked himself up from the ditch, wiped off the snow and mud from his tunic and then began to sing all over again! And he, like a real troubadour of the Lord, never stopped singing. The joy he found in Christ was too much for him to keep locked up inside.

A Net That Draws Souls to God

Anyone who loves sports knows that in order to win, you need both a good offense and a good defense. One without the other is not enough for victory. For example, in baseball you need good hitters to score a lot of runs; that's a good offense in baseball. But if you do not have good pitching and good fielding, the other team will score more runs and win. You can lose without a good defense. Or take football or basketball, for example. You can have a team that plays good defense, keeping the other team from scoring too many points; that's very important for victory. But if the offense scores even fewer points because the other team has a better defense, the team will lose for lack of scoring.

Just as a good defense and a good offense go together in sports, so they must go together in the work of drawing people to the Lord. We live a life of virtue for ourselves, of course, so that we are holy and pleasing to the Lord. In this, joy is a good "defense," helping us to live personally satisfying lives. We also live righteous and prayerful lives so that we are able to participate in the great work of evangelization that is the responsibility of each and every Christian. In this, we use joy as our "offense," because it is a powerful tool for evangelization.

Spiritual joy affects not only the evangelizer, but also

those being evangelized. Mother Teresa was a very joyful person who understood the effectiveness of joy in dealing with others. On my first visit to the Missionaries of Charity in the South Bronx, I saw a poster that read, "Joy is the surest sign of God's presence in the soul." If we say that a person's face is the window of his soul, then a joyful look, a kind smile, unmistakably reflects God's presence within. Without God in the soul, we cannot have love, joy or peace within. This is why Saint Paul can write: "For the kingdom of God is not food and drink but righteousness and peace and joy in the Holy Spirit" (Romans 14:17, NRSV).

Mother Teresa was certainly someone in whom we could see the joy of God's presence radiating out to others, even to the poorest of the poor. This is why so many people of different social, cultural, ethnic and even religious backgrounds were attracted to her. She valued joy so much that she made "cheerfulness" part of the charism or spirit of her community, the Missionaries of Charity.

Mother Teresa used to say that a joyful servant of God is a net to catch souls for God. With so much drudgery and unhappiness in the world today, authentically joyful persons stand out. Other people will stop and take notice, especially if it is a quality they lack but wish they could find for themselves. When they discover the joy they are looking for staring back at them in the face of another, they are drawn like a fish to the bait on the hook.

Mother Teresa also said that a joyful servant of God preaches without preaching. If a picture is worth a thousand words, who can measure the effect of a joyful believer on others, believers and nonbelievers alike?

I experienced the powerful attraction of joy when I was a young teenager thinking of entering the seminary. I visited a friary where there were a number of young brothers in training. I thoroughly enjoyed my day with them. I remember coming home from my visit that day, and thinking to myself, "I want that happiness for myself!"

The best thing any salesperson can do to sell his or her product is to tell customers, "I use the product myself, and I like it!" The joyfulness of an evangelist tells all that and more before he even utters a word!

Humor and Holiness

An important part of Mother Teresa's joyfulness was her wonderful sense of humor. On one occasion she said to me, "Father, I have a new prayer. I pray to God: 'Use me. Do whatever you want with my life. Send me wherever you want. But don't consult me!'"

It is important for Christians to have a good sense of humor and a good wit. For one thing, people more easily remember things said with humor. After all, the only creatures that God made in this world that have a sense of humor and can laugh are human beings. So, humor must be a very important quality.

Humor and wit can often mean the difference between a positive discussion ending on a good note and a harsh argument ending on a bad note of anger or hurt feelings. I once heard a story from the life of Archbishop Sheen that illustrates this. He was on a train when he got into a discussion with an Episcopal priest about the validity of Anglican orders. (The Catholic Church does not accept the validity of those orders.) The archbishop presented the Catholic position, while the priest defended his belief that his orders were valid. A sizable crowd gathered in the train, and the discussion started to get a bit tense.

Finally, when the train came to a certain stop, the Episcopal priest got off. But still continuing the discussion from the station platform, the priest said to the archbishop through the open window of the train, "Archbishop Sheen, my orders are as valid as yours. I am as much a priest as you are! There's nothing you can do that I cannot do also."

Archbishop Sheen responded with great wit, "Well, I can kiss your wife, but you can't kiss mine!" I'm sure everyone got a good laugh out of that remark, including the Episcopal priest!

We should be aware that often people respond initially more to how we relate to them, to our openness and acceptance of them, than to our message. Once they believe we accept and respect them, they will be much more open to listening to what we have to say. Here is where kindness and especially cheerfulness can do wonders. Where a frown or just an overly serious expression may scare off potential inquirers, a kind and easy smile will be very welcoming. As another great evangelist in Church history, Saint Francis de Sales, used to say, we will attract more bees with an ounce of honey than a barrel of vinegar.

Saint Teresa of Avila famously prayed: "From sour-faced saints, O Lord, deliver us." We can echo that prayer in support of the Church's evangelization mission: "From sour-faced evangelists, O Lord, deliver us." A bad impression, once made, can easily become a lasting impression, especially for persons who already have a negative image or high degree of suspicion about the Catholic Church. So as a popular saying puts it, "If you are happy, please remember to inform your face." They say it takes more facial muscles to frown than to smile, so why would we want to overwork ourselves for the wrong results?

Joy is our secret weapon in the Christian life and in our work of evangelization. Jesus gave this gift to us at the Last Supper: "These things I have spoken to you, that my joy may be in you, and that your joy may be full" (John 15:11). The Holy Spirit produces joy in us as one of His fruits (Galatians 5:22). When Christians are filled with the Lord's joy and communicate that joy to others, we have the total defense and offense together.

May God's Church be filled with prayerful, virtuous Christians who carry their crosses joyfully in union with Jesus. Through their faithful witness may all men and women and children come to know the love and mercy of God!

Chapter Two: Have You Had Your Hour of Power Today?
The Importance of Making a Holy Hour
1. First Message of His Holiness Benedict XVI at the End of the Eucharistic Concelebration with the Members of the College of Cardinals in the Sistine Chapel, April 20, 2005, www.vatican.va.

Chapter Seven: Discerning God's Will
1. John Henry Newman, *Meditations and Devotions* (Harrison, N.Y.: Roman Catholic, 1995), pp. 6–7.

Chapter Nine: When God Says Yes to Our Prayers
1. Prayer of a Civil War Soldier, www.cathmsa.org.

Chapter Fourteen: Building the Civilization of Love by Our Deeds of Charity
1. From a letter by Saint Peter Claver, May 31, 1672, quoted in Spanish in A. Valtierra, *Saint Peter Claver* (Cartagena, 1964), pp. 140–141. *The Liturgy of the Hours According to the Roman Rite,* volume 4 (New York: Catholic Book, 1975), pp. 2016–2017.

Chapter Seventeen: The Suffering That Redeems Souls
1. Sister Lucia, *Fatima in Lucia's Own Words,* Louis Kondor, ed., Dominican Nuns of Perpetual Rosary, trans. (Cambridge, Mass.: Ravensgate, 1976), pp. 108, 171.

2. Sister Lucia, pp. 167–169, 172. Prayer adapted by the author to reflect common usage.

3. Sister Lucia, p. 64.

4. Sister Lucia, p. 165.

Chapter Nineteen: What Might My Cross Look Like?
1. www.catholic.org.

Chapter Twenty-One: The Heart of Mary
1. Saint John Chrysostom, *The Liturgy of the Hours According to the Roman Rite,* volume 3 (New York: Catholic Book, 1975), pp. 1646–1647.

2. www.catholic.org.

Chapter Twenty-Two: Joy: An Important Safeguard for Our Spiritual Lives
1. Friedrich Nietzsche, *Thus Spake Zarathustra,* Thomas Common, trans., www.fordham.edu.